P9-CRA-257

Nordic Folk Churches

Nordic Folk Churches

A CONTEMPORARY CHURCH HISTORY

Björn Ryman

with

Aila Lauha

Gunnar Heiene

&

Peter Lodberg

William B. Eerdmans Publishing Company

Grand Rapids, Michigan / Cambridge, U.K.

© 2005 Wm. B. Eerdmans Publishing Co.
All rights reserved

Wm. B. Eerdmans Publishing Co.
255 Jefferson Ave. S.E.,
Grand Rapids, Michigan 49503 /
P.O. Box 163, Cambridge CB3 9PU U.K.

Printed in the United States of America

10 09 08 07 06 05   7 6 5 4 3 2 1

ISBN 0-8028-2879-5

ISSN 1652-8581
FORSKNING FÖR KYRKAN 2, Svenska Kyrkan

www.eerdmans.com

Contents

Contents

Foreword

Every presentation of church history must reflect tradition and transformation. It belongs to the key characteristic of Protestant churches to be in transition, to reflect the pilgrim nature of the community of faith. It is always easier to describe a product than a process, which is why perceptions of churches are so varied and history writing so full of surprises. The reader adds to the complexities of interpretation, and the closer the reader is to the events, the more complex the interpretation.

My perspective on this presentation of contemporary Nordic church life is both as an insider — an ordained pastor and bishop of the Church of Norway — and as an ecumenist with a perspective from Geneva.

The Nordic churches have been among the founders and staunchest supporters of the World Council of Churches, the Lutheran World Federation, and the Conference of European Churches. In many ways they speak and act with one voice, but there are also significant variations on a broad scale of issues. This is demonstrated by the status reports these churches' bishops give every third year when all the Nordic bishops convene for a four-day conference. The report from the Danish folk church includes Greenland and the Faroe Islands. The Nordic Bishops Conference is a nonformal gathering that makes no decisions — except for where to meet next. This creates a sense of collegiality and a relaxed exchange of views, even on the most controversial issues. Thus, at the meeting at the end of June 2004 in Porvoo, Finland, the bishops — and their spouses — shared insights and concerns on many diverse issues. How do demographic changes and rapid urbanization affect the numbers of those being baptized and confirmed? What are the liturgical developments in the regular services of the church? How are the traditional ecumenical challenges affecting inter-Nordic church relations, and how do we as churches overcome xenophobia and racism within church and society? If you add to this such themes as the Nordic churches and the European Union and the global challenge of HIV/AIDS, you get a pretty good sense of how Nordic bishops interpret their role and place in church and society. A gathering of Nordic bishops is characterized by its worship life, including Bible studies, which again bring out a shared spirituality and ethos through church-specific traditions. With the demise of the Nordic Ecumenical Council, this structure has perhaps gained new importance as a meeting point.

As general secretary of the Lutheran World Federation (1985-94), I sometimes missed a coherent and concise presentation of the member churches in the North. The "established churches," i.e., the state and folk churches in Denmark, Sweden, Finland, Norway, and Iceland, form a very important part of the global family of Lutheran churches. This is seen in the fields of theology, mission, international *diaconia*, human rights, peace, and many other vital aspects of the global church. The place and role of women in church and society has effectively been promoted by these churches. The churches of Sweden, Denmark, and Norway each have two women as bishops. The ratio of women to men in students preparing for the ministry is fifty-fifty. Youth have generally played a more visible role than in many other member churches of the Lutheran communion, increasingly also in decision-making bodies. Lay movements have contributed importantly to the spiritual formation, and in those churches that have synodical structures they form the majority in the decision-making bodies.

Within the *oikoumene* there exists a variety of interpretations regarding the identity and characteristics of these Nordic churches. If I try to stereotype, I would suggest the following reading from my Geneva vantage point: German Lutheran churches tend to regard the Nordic Lutherans as cousins who have more or less strayed away from important elements of the family heritage, they themselves being the only true custodians of an undiluted Lutheran heritage. Sister churches on the North American continent seem to look somewhat askance at these hybrids of state churches. Nor is their life as folk churches much appreciated by third- and fourth-generation immigrants from this region to the United States and Canada.

Among the churches in the South, the "mother churches" are held in high regard because of their history of mission and relief, but not without a sense of resentment because of a perceived paternalism. Lately there has emerged a more critical tone, sometimes in rather harsh words from church leaders in the South on what is perceived as secularization, the bondage of the churches to the state, and especially on the issue of ordination of people who live in same-sex unions.

In some of these exchanges the issue boils down to the perennial question of how to read the Bible as a source of faith and life in a modern age. Certainly these stereotypes all contain some elements of truth. But the picture of Nordic Lutheranism is of course more complex. There are also variations between these churches, inter alia, on ecclesiology and ministry. In terms of church-state relations there are significant variations, with Denmark and Finland at opposite ends of the spectrum. On a traditional conservative-liberal scale, one might see the Finnish church as the most conservative among the Nordic majority churches, perhaps influenced by the presence of the second official church in the nation, the Finnish Orthodox Church. In matters of human rights, highlighted in the struggle against racism, these churches have spoken and acted in concert, although some with a clearer voice than others. I believe it is right to say that the churches of Sweden and of Norway have been in the vanguard in the struggle for peace and justice, beginning with such towering figures from the first half of the twentieth century as Nathan Söderblom and Eivind Berggrav, both of whom connected ecumenism inextricably to the work for peace and reconciliation. The Danish folk church has most consistently projected ambivalence with regard to the political ministry of the church. But there is also a wind of change in this church. This is affecting the church-state issue — although disestablishment is not on the horizon — and it is clearly noticeable in the realm of social ethics, or as some would term it, the political mandate of the church.

Ecumenically, these churches are not as like-minded as they are perceived to be from the outside. The Porvoo Agreement signed in 1995 brought together the Anglican churches in England, Scotland, Ireland, and Wales and the Lutheran majority churches in the Nordic region and the Lutheran churches in Estonia and Lithuania. The Danes, together with the Lutheran Church in Latvia, have not joined the Porvoo fellowship, due to an inherent fear of anything "high church." It is especially the Anglo-Catholic interpretation of the office of the bishop that is irreconcilable with the classical Danish reading of Lutheran ecclesiology and ministry. They have, on the other hand, recently joined the Reformed-dominated Leuenberg fellowship.

A certain preoccupation with the idea of apostolic succession is characteristic of the Church of Sweden, earning her a privileged position at the papal court. Women in the church and other gender-related issues, such as ordination of homosexuals, are causing a persistent cold wind to blow from the Vatican toward the north, however. The signing in 1997 by the Vatican Secretariat for Christian Unity and the Lutheran World Federation of the Joint Declaration on Justification testifies to a greater ecumenical vision in the relationship between these two historically antagonistic faith communities, even if they still are a long way from a common view on such issues as ecclesiology, ministry, and authority. Social issues are as divisive as before, not least because of such theological issues as anthropology and sacraments. Such a diversity and asymmetry of ecumenical relationships has however not had any noticeable negative effect on the inner-Nordic sense of belonging to each other.

The Nordic churches — which are incorrectly termed the Scandinavian churches — have played a significant role in the nation building of their respective countries. Without exception, they have, as majority churches, formed the spiritual, cultural, and social foundation during more than a thousand years of intertwined nation, state, and church history. The texture of the Nordic welfare state is unambiguously Christian.

Within the United Nations and generally in foreign policy, the spiritual and moral legacy of Christian faith on these northern shores of Europe is clearly reflected.

This timely book presents to a larger readership an important study project of the transformation process of Nordic folk churches. The reader will find information and analysis that helps explain where these churches have come from and where they are now. Its thematic approach invites the reader to reflect on theological issues of great significance to the church in a dominantly secular, pluralistic, multicultural, and multireligious region. A selection of biographies of national heroes, in chapter 9, reminds the reader of the confluence of politics and church history in an overwhelmingly Protestant environment. The theology, history, and daily life of these churches is a compelling testimony to the church as a spiritual, sacramental, confessional, and witnessing communion in words and deeds. It also is a constant reminder of the vulnerability of the church as an organization. But above all, we are made aware of the uniqueness of the church as an organism, as a communion of faith — as a part of the one, holy, and apostolic church. The Nordic churches reflect in a small measure the diversity that has to be reconciled for the church in the world to be seen and believed as the *Una Sancta*. This presentation brings us to the gray zone between history and journalism arguing the truth of the old Lutheran dictum *ecclesia semper reformanda*.

BISHOP GUNNAR STÅLSETT

Introduction

BJÖRN RYMAN

What is Nordic and what is the meaning of folk churches? Visitors to the Scandinavian countries might not grasp the essence of the Nordic folk churches. Students of theology or history find very little in print in the English language about the modern history of the Nordic folk churches. Scholars of contemporary history have access only to limited sources, as most of these sources are in a language foreign to them.

This volume in contemporary church history fills a knowledge gap both about the Nordic churches and about their contribution to the modern ecumenical movement. It might also offer new insights into recent developments in the Nordic countries. This volume in English is a spin-off of a research project conducted by thirty Nordic church historians. The result of that project was a 500-page volume: *Nordiske Folkekirker i opbrud. National identitet og international nyorientering efter 1945* (Nordic folk churches breaking up: National identity and the new international agenda after 1945) (Aarhus Universitetsforlag, 2001). That project was part of a large-scale research program initiated by the Nordic Council of Ministers, titled "The Nordic Countries and Europe." The church historians under the leadership of Professor Jens Holger Schjørring (Aarhus) took a comparative approach to the relationship of the Nordic folk churches to European development. What is common in the Nordic heritage? What are the similarities between the folk churches in Denmark,

Finland, Iceland, Norway, and Sweden? Have they developed differently than the rest of Europe in the postwar period? In the forty-five chapters of the book, new research is published on the period 1945-70 on seven different themes:

1. Realistic images after the war
2. Folk church — emergency aid — welfare
3. The church order and the political parties
4. Revival movements in a secularized age
5. Church and school in a pluralistic society
6. Folk church, ecumenics, and internationalization
7. A new theological approach about the folk church

Bracketing the special contributions by the thirty church historians are a lengthy introduction and a short conclusion by Professor Schjørring, who places the research in a comparative European theological setting. The volume you hold in your hands cannot do justice to all of this particular research. As empirical research is sometimes very detailed, this volume is a synthesis and might look superficial. Our approach, however, is comparative and historical. Recent developments are viewed in a historical context. We try to see the Nordic churches as an entity. The book is written to allow an outsider without particular prior knowledge of the Nordic churches to follow the text. Compared with the original book, we have left out many details relating to theologians and politicians, well-known in their respective countries. Few names are mentioned. We decided to portray only some of the Nordic church leaders and political leaders and put them in the context of the folk churches.

The period covered is from the Second World War until the turn of the millennium. An introductory chapter gives a historical thousand-year sketch of the Nordic churches from the coming of Christianity until the Second World War. Next the authors outline the development in each country. Then three themes are followed in a contextual way: the ecumenical world, church and society, and theology and spirituality. Some of the key words in this process are "modernization," "globalization," and "welfare societies." Have the Nordic churches been salt or mirror in this development? How have they coped? Is the Nordic church development much different today compared to other European countries? Special emphasis is laid on events and personalities that influenced the international and ecumenical scene.

For specialists in church history we recommend the original book.

1. Nordic Churches from 1000 to 1940

Björn Ryman

A tourist to the Cathedral of Uppsala exclaims: "This church looks like a Catholic church! I always thought Sweden was a Protestant country."

Yes, all the Nordic countries have been Protestant since the beginning of the sixteenth century. The Lutheran Reformation reached Scandinavia very quickly. Already in the 1520s, decisions in this direction were being made by the national diets. By that time most parts of the Nordic countries had been Roman Catholic for half a millennium. This period of history — the Middle Ages — is characterized by allegiance to the Roman Catholic Church and the pope in Rome. The Nordic countries were gradually being Christianized through missionary efforts from the south and the west, as well as from travel and intercommunication. This put its mark on the Nordic countries. Many of the churches being used today were built during the Middle Ages. That architecture, both Roman and Gothic, is well preserved. So are many of the art treasures: sculptures of the virgin Mary and of kings who were hero-saints, altar pictures, mural paintings — thanks to the cold climate and minimal plundering, most of the art pieces are still intact. Even textiles from the fourteenth century are still there. The Reformation never brought the iconoclast to the Nordic countries. That is why the cathedrals and parish churches to some extent may look Catholic.

The first known missionary to Denmark and Sweden came from the

1

The millennial commemoration of the first baptism of a Swedish king in Husaby was attended by church representatives from Germany and Britain, which sent missionaries to the Nordic countries. Those seated in the front row include Bishop Arborelius of the Roman Catholic diocese of Stockholm and the first female bishop in Sweden, Christina Odenberg, appointed 1997.
Photo: Jim Elfström, IKON.

northern part of Germany. His name was Ansgar, and he was so successful that he was made bishop of Hamburg, which diocese included all of
Scandinavia. He arrived at the island of Birka, close to present-day
Stockholm, in 829 and was received by the king. Both the trading town
of Birka and the congregation Ansgar founded vanished, and the mission from the south was only partially successful. But missionaries from
the British Isles a couple centuries later, at the end of the age of the Vikings in the eleventh century, were more successful. Some of these, like
Botwid, Eskil, David, and Sigfrid, were canonized. So the Christian influences on Scandinavia came from both Germany and Britain.

The missionary strategy was to reach the kings and their earls. This
top-down approach in mission also determined when a nation was considered Christian: when the king and all his men had received baptism,
the nation was considered Christian. This occurred first in Denmark,
followed by Norway around 950. The Swedish king Olof was baptized
around the year 1000. All of Iceland gathered in 1000 and unanimously
decided to adopt Christianity. The decision-making body was called
Allthing, which is still the name of the Icelandic parliament.

The Viking age was an era of expansion for the Danish, Norwegian,
and Swedish people. Considered traders by some, terrorists by others,
the Vikings reached very far: in the west to Iceland, Greenland, and
North America; in the east deep into Russia and all the way to Constantinople. In the south they plundered many cloisters and burned cities.
"From the fury of the Norsemen, save us, dear God," victims prayed in
Normandy. The missionary efforts were undoubtedly spurred by the
victims of this terrorist fury. On the other hand, the Vikings were the
main traders of this period, when the Mediterranean Sea was dominated
by Muslim powers, and as such they probably took Christians as slaves
back to the Nordic countries, particularly from the Slavic people. Our
word for slave stems from this period. Some Vikings settled in Christian
countries, particularly in Norfolk, Britain, and Normandy, France. Their
children might have returned to the country of their parents and taken
the Christian faith with them.

By 1000 Christianity was established in Denmark, Norway, Iceland,
and Sweden. Of course, practices from the old Norse religion continued,

including worship of the old gods of Oden, Thor, Frey, and many others. Their names are still alive in the names of our weekdays: Wednesday (*onsdag*), Thursday, and Friday. There was an inculturization when the old Norse religion met the Roman Catholic version of Christianity. The old places of pagan worship were turned into Christian worship places, where churches were built. This is true of the Jelling Stone of Denmark as well as Old Uppsala of Sweden. The old religion was not physically destroyed but replaced by Christianity, and gradually new forms of worship developed.

Christianity reached Finland later than the other countries, and influences came from both the East and the West. The Russian Orthodox Church had some influence on Finland and also reached into eastern Sweden. The king of Sweden organized crusades to Finland around 1150, and Finland came under Swedish influence and remained so until 1809, when Russian influence prevailed. In the region close to the border between Russia and Finland, Western and Eastern types of Christianity coexisted. The border has changed many times through history as Finland has been a battlefield for many wars between Sweden and Russia. Some of the Swedish crusades also went to Estonia, although Estonia was more influenced by Germany than by Sweden. Estonia and Livonia had to accept the Western mode of Christianity, and this meant that the Baltic Sea was surrounded by countries of the Western type of Christianity.

The three main centers for the church in the North were Lund for Denmark, including southern Sweden (established 1103); Trondheim for Norway (1153); and Uppsala for Sweden and Finland (1164). In Finland a bishop of Åbo was established in 1229, which is today the see of the archbishop of the Finnish church. Cathedrals were erected, and are still standing and being used. The three provinces claimed allegiance both to Rome and to the national kingdoms that were evolving slowly into states and nations. The church everywhere was organized into dioceses and parishes, and bishops were appointed in every cathedral city. These appointments were usually in congruence with the royal power; otherwise there was the threat of a battle between the worldly and the spiritual powers. The territorial parish system was extended throughout the realm. The parish churches, which were erected and paid for by the peasants, and the parish borders that were established are in many cases still valid today.

Although the church provinces in the North were guided by Rome, they gradually developed into national churches, and were established as such, with territorial parishes, long before the Reformation. Church and politics were intermingled long before the sovereign kings laid their hands on the churches. The embryo of the national folk churches was already there, although the churches were part of the church universal. Signs of this embryonic movement were: the church buildings, the territorial parish with all inhabitants included as baptized members, the bishops as heads of dioceses with a chapter in each cathedral city, and the kings and their councils themselves being Christian and defending the Christian faith.

In the middle of the twelfth century, monks and nuns from Germany, France, and Britain established religious orders in the Scandinavian countries. In addition to strengthening Christianity, they brought with them a new culture. Physically they introduced new herbs, new agricultural methods, new breeds of horses, splendid architecture, new cuisine, the art of writing and illuminating parchment books, glorious singing, and medical first aid. Most of the European orders were established, like the Cistercians, Dominicans, and Franciscans. In one sense they managed to make the Nordic countries European, convincing them to adopt their culture and abstain from the barbaric mores of their Nordic ancestors. But literacy and education were still the exclusive privilege of a few church people. Many students from the Nordic countries pursued their higher education at the universities of Paris and Bologna. The height of European influence was the founding of the University of Uppsala in 1477 and the University of Copenhagen in 1478.

The population density was very low in the Nordic countries: it was highest in Denmark and lowest in Finland. The deep forests of Finland, Norway, and Sweden were considered dangerous places. The plains were suited for agriculture, and that's where most of the people settled and the churches and monasteries were built. Income from agriculture financed both the kings and their armies as well as the parishes and the monasteries. Most cathedrals were erected in the agriculturally rich re-

In Nordic countries, hundreds of medieval churches are still used as parish churches. A runic stone with a Christian cross from the eleventh century gives evidence of the acceptance of Christianity.
Photo: Jim Elfström, IKON.

gions. In Denmark particularly, the nobility dominated the agricultural scene and owned much land. In the forests in Finland, Norway, and Sweden, freeholding farms were established and the influence of the nobility was not as great. People were scarce, however, particularly during the century after the bubonic plague, also called the Black Death, which diminished the population by one-third or more. Norway was hardest hit; its nobility was wiped out and the nation came under the influence of the Danish king. Scandinavia as a whole was never feudalistic in the same way as other parts of Europe. One reason was that so many farmers owned their own land. Their tax burden to the king to cover costs for wars was sometimes so heavy that they revolted. The peasants became so influential that they were represented in the Swedish and Danish diets in the middle of the fifteenth century, when the four estates of nobility, clergy, burghers, and farmers met for the first time. The local parish depended on the freeholding farmers for the upkeep of the parish church and the support of the parish priest.

One nation, one law, and one faith — this became true for the Scandinavian countries. All inhabitants had to belong to the church. Bishops were in some cases as much worldly powerful politicians as spiritual leaders. This was one reason for reforming the church. Another emanated from the richness of the church as a landholder, especially the cloisters. Some of them were large enterprises, being the biggest landholder in their region. The cloister of Vadstena was founded by Saint Birgitta (1303-73). That is the only religious order originating from Scandinavia. Birgitta came from an influential Swedish family and was a widow when she started having revelations — the *Revelationes Birgittae*. These encompassed spiritual guidance, moral advice, and political programs for kings and popes. Seven hundred years after her birth — 2003 — she was considered patron saint of Europe and celebrated by Swedish Lutherans and Roman Catholics in an ecumenical spirit. Her lasting contribution, the nunnery at Vadstena, was again made a cloister in the twentieth century.

During the fifteenth century all of the Nordic North was in a political union, the Kalmarunionen, decided upon by the nobility and the bishops. Territorially it was the largest kingdom of Europe, running from the Arctic Circle down to present-day Germany and from Greenland to the Russian border. Strife among the nobility led to civil wars and an economic decline. The hostility was deepest between the Swedish nobility and the Danish king, who as the legally appointed king had the support of the pope. These experiences were some of the reasons all of Scandinavia, and particularly Stockholm, the capital of Sweden, was ripe for the ideas of the Reformation.

Martin Luther's ideas, both in writing and in sermons, reached Scandinavia quickly. Already by 1523, Luther's theology had found its way to Stockholm and the new king, Gustavus Vasa, by way of Olaus Petri, one of Luther's students. The fact that the new ideas from Wittenberg traveled so fast says something of how ripe Sweden was politically and theologically for the new teachings. They gave the Swedish king an excuse for breaking with the pope and the Danish king as head of the Nordic union. He showed no hesitance in taking land and silver from the church. Cloisters were abandoned and demolished. The Reformation was a convenient vehicle for strengthening the central power of the king. It also gave the theologians a better opportunity to preach in Swedish, read the Bible in Swedish, and sing hymns from the new hymnbook. The printing press served the spread of the Reformation well. Already in 1526 the hymnal and the New Testament were printed in Swedish. The whole Bible was translated and printed in 1541 as the king's version. This practice of considering the Bible translation as a national concern has been repeated until this day — the latest publicly sponsored translation coming in 2000. In 1526 they followed to a great extent Luther's German translation, which made Swedish written language become similar to German.

In Finland the great reformer was Mikael Agricola, who also translated the Bible into Finnish. He was an author of theological books and maybe the most influential Finnish theologian ever. He managed to synthesize Finnish language, culture, and religion. In other respects Finland was part of Sweden and organized its two dioceses and parishes in the same way as Sweden. The same church order was used. Finnish clergy and farmers were represented in the diet *(riksdag)* in Sweden.

The brother of Olaus Petri, Laurentius, was appointed archbishop in 1531 and remained so until 1572. He worked out the liturgy for the churches in Sweden and Finland, which kept many of the practices from the Catholic order. He also established the episcopal order with an archbishop in Uppsala and bishops as heads of dioceses. The Swedish church was saved from royal excess. However, the king had a say in appointments of bishops and clergy, and his influence created close church-state relationships for several centuries to come. Theology and politics walked hand in hand. The power of the pope in Rome had been replaced by the power of the king.

In Denmark-Norway the Reformation came a little later, due to political circumstances. By the time the Reformation was established in neighboring Sweden as well as in the northern provinces of Germany, bordering Denmark, the king and the country were ready for it. The year 1536 was decisive, and the king was influential in bringing it about. Johannes Bugenhagen is considered the Danish religious Reformer. This made almost all of northern Europe evangelical/Lutheran in confession, which had a great impact on language, culture, education, mentality, and the shaping of the political institutions. As we have seen in this brief introduction, shifts in religion in Scandinavia have been collective in character from the king down to the people. This was true both for the Reformation and the acceptance of Christianity five hundred years earlier. Of course, there were exceptions: bishops loyal to Rome going into exile, clergymen and noble families using Catholic rituals in secret, etc. Not until 1600 were the countries completely Lutheran in teaching and in practice.

The age of confessionalism is an appropriate name for the centuries that followed. The main Lutheran confessional statement from 1530, Confessio Augustana, was accepted as the teaching of the nation. Ideologically the Scandinavian countries were linked to the European principalities where Lutheran doctrine was taught, which meant northern Germany. Ordinary people learned Martin Luther's small catechism by heart from childhood onward. The people were homogenized into the same uniform way of thinking. It was considered a duty to attend Sunday service, and all rites of life from baptism of the newly born to burial were the same for all. State and church became intertwined, and harsh punishments were handed down for what we today consider private matters. This age never saw religion or morals as private. The ideological framework for each individual and all of society was the teaching of the three estates: the political order = the nobility; the teaching order = the clergy; the household order = the peasants. Each individual should belong to a collective household, which resembles the idea of the extended family in Africa. The head of the household was the farmer. He got the authority from God and the king to exercise discipline, but also to look after the welfare of everyone in his house. This is why some prefer to call this order patriarchal. Luther based his catechism on this order. This mentality reigned for three centuries. It gave the parish pastor a strong position in society. He was also a man of the state, serving the king. He systematically examined young and old from every household in how well they could read the Bible and understand the catechism. He was also a guardian of private and public morality, particularly around marriage. The custom in the North of relatively high marriage age for women made it easier for the peasants to preserve the family farms and keep stability.

Formal population records were kept, which have been preserved and show an amazingly high literacy rate among the peasants. It was highest in the farms closest to the church and lowest in the outskirts of the parish. Before primary education became compulsory in the nineteenth century, the ability to read and write was widespread in Scandinavia. The church was also responsible for introducing new methods of public health, like smallpox vaccination, and agriculture, like potato planting. The churches kept population records long before the public census was established. Church and state went hand in hand in organizing the people, and no one saw any demarcation line between the two.

The kings of Denmark and Sweden saw themselves as defenders of Protestantism in Europe against Catholicism. The height of this religious war was from 1618 to 1648, when Germany was a battlefield for foreign troops, and lost half its population. Sweden was a victor on the Protestant side and Denmark was a loser, foremost to its rival Sweden. As a great power, Sweden had the ambition of making the Baltic Sea a Swedish sea, which caused many wars to take place in Poland, Russia, and the Baltic provinces. Russia also became a great power with its enormous landmass and was a constant threat to Finland. Six wars were fought between Russia and Sweden, many of them on Finnish soil. Sweden with its center in Stockholm was geared eastward, while Denmark with its center in Copenhagen looked westward to the Atlantic. A western type of Lutheranism developed in Denmark, Norway, and Iceland, and an eastern type in Sweden and Finland. As a consequence of the Westphalian peace treaty of 1648, which gave kings the right to decide the religious practice in their realm, Sweden and Denmark remained firm in Lutheranism. Another consequence of this peace was the freedom for the smaller states to develop into nation-states. The power of the emperor and the pope was definitely broken for northern Europe. In this way the nations of Denmark and Sweden developed strong links to their subjects, shaping them for nationalism as a force for nation building.

Lutheranism was the glue that kept societies together in the Nordic countries. Another rite was gradually introduced from the 1720s on: confirmation of young people, girls and boys alike. As in the Anglican Church, it rapidly became a compulsory ritual in every parish. "Compulsion" is a key word today when thinking about this age, but most people of those days saw religious life as practiced as a natural way of life and the best for society. When individualism and enlightenment entered Scandinavia in the eighteenth century, conflicts arose. Pietism from Halle was introduced around 1700 and found adherents among the upper classes who saw a spiritual renewal coming. In Denmark the royal family was greatly impressed and sponsored the sending of missionaries to India. In Sweden, however, it was suppressed by orthodox Lutheranism creating special laws against private convocations. The lid was so tight that an explosion occurred when revivals on a mass scale hit Scandinavia around 1850.

Orthodox theology, although stern on new teachings, did accept new inventions made by natural science. In this area stern Lutheranism showed a tolerant and progressive side, and there was no opposition to the scientific discoveries made during this time. The astronomer Tycho Brahe from Denmark started the revolution of astronomy. In Uppsala, sons of clergy like Carolus Linnaeus systematized the flora (1740) and

11

Anders Celsius gave us the thermometer (1740). Another example, in economics, is the Finnish clergyman Anders Chydenius (1729-1803), a vicar in the far north. As a member of Parliament in Stockholm in 1765, he argued strongly for the liberal ideas of free trade, freedom of religion, and a market economy. His economic ideas were ahead of Adam Smith in Britain. As a pietistic Lutheran vicar at a poor congregation in the periphery, his driving force was the empowerment of his people against the capital accumulation in the center of the nation.

In the nineteenth century, Scandinavia was influenced by new ideas of liberalism, tolerance, socialism, rationalism, positivism, etc. Old society and its form of government vanished. New religious ideas coming from England took hold. Methodism and Baptist teachings were introduced. High literacy rates prepared people not only to read the Bible but to draw their own conclusions. Lay preachers outside the Nordic churches became popular. New associations got started, evolving into congregations and eventually into free churches. The associations empowered the laypeople, especially the women, and gave them a new role in society. These new movements of the people were a foundation stone for the modern emerging society.

In Denmark, all this took place inside the folk church. Thanks to the great thinker and reformer Nicolaus Grundtvig, this revival was both religious and national in character and included particularly the poor peasants. The movement of farmers became well organized, politically to the left, organizationally cooperative in character, and intellectually based on Grundtvig's idea of people's high school. As Denmark experienced a political change in 1848-49 with a new written constitution and wars against the new Germany, nationalism and religion forged a new alliance.

The same was true of Norway, which had been in forced political alliance with Sweden since 1814. That year Norway wrote its constitution, considered most liberal in Europe, and freed itself from Denmark. The union with Sweden was not so tight, and on the church level there was little influence. On the other hand, Norway had a great awakening of its own, led by a lay preacher, Hans Nielsen Hauge. Prayer chapels with lay preachers were established in most places. Christian associations, pietistic in character, were established with strong ties between the members. The members remained churchgoers in the parish church but were activists in the chapel of the revival. This evolved sociologically into an ellipse structure.

In Finland the pietistic revival movements were as strong as in Denmark and Norway. There arose three distinct movements centered around charismatic leaders of the revival. Finland was, during the nineteenth century, an autonomous principality under the Russian czar in Saint Petersburg. Czarist rule was not as tough as anticipated and led to a certain self-governance of the Lutheran church in 1869 with a new church law, as Russia favored the Orthodox Church under the czar. Because of this, Finnish state-church relations were at another level than in the other Nordic countries. Politically, Finland experienced traumatic changes in the twentieth century. The shifts were sudden and violent. After the Communist revolution in Russia, Finland declared itself independent in 1917. A civil war broke out between the "reds" and the "whites." Finland established a modern parliamentary government, where the official church still had a strong position among the population.

In Sweden, several local revivals took place among the farmers, many of them led by clergymen who remained within the church but developed distinct methods of behavior and preaching. Other revivals were led by lay preachers, and this caused legal actions to be brought against them. Methodism and Baptist teachings, and later the Salvation Army, were imports from England. They became free churches, and the religious map of Sweden resembled that of Britain. Denominations existed side by side with the large Church of Sweden, which identified itself as a church for all the people within the territory — a folk church.

Language became a political issue as the central power exercised its authority through dictating which language should be used. Stockholm decided the form of Swedish that should be written and spoken officially in all of Sweden and Finland. Copenhagen extended its Danish to all of Denmark, Norway, Iceland, and the Faroe Islands. The Icelanders kept their original Nordic language but had to learn Danish as well. The Norwegians had to use Danish. Around 1860, as part of the nationalistic

The Sami, most of whom live in Norway, worship in their own language, and a new liturgy has recently taken shape.   Photo: Jim Elfström, IKON.

movement, an original version of Norwegian dialect, called New Norwegian, was developed into written language. As an independent nation, Norway uses both forms.

Finnish has no connection to the other Nordic languages. It is a language on its own, developed into a written language during the Reformation. Swedish was used officially in courts and schools. Educated people spoke Swedish. A shift occurred with the nationalistic movement, which demanded Finnish to be the main language. Officially Finland still uses both languages, but less than 5 percent of the population uses Swedish as its mother tongue.

The Sami people have lived close to the Arctic Circle for ages. Of the fifty thousand Samis, the majority reside in Norway. Since around 1500 the reindeer has been most vital to their livelihood. The Samis developed a nomadic lifestyle, moving between the rough mountains and the deep forests. They had their mode of worship with drums and shamans. As the central power extended its influence, the Samis felt colonized and maltreated as an indigenous people. There were Christians among them already in 1300. From the eighteenth century the central power regulated their activities through schools. Their local languages and customs were suppressed. They were forced to speak Norwegian or Swedish. Many were drawn into the awakening in 1844, led by Laestadius, vicar of the northernmost parish of Sweden. Racism and land grabbing from settlers hurt them badly. Not until recently have the churches recognized their guilt in this process. A reconciliatory process is ongoing, including the recognition of the Sami culture in Christian worship.

The twentieth century gradually developed secularized societies. Churches were more and more marginalized in the age of rapid industrialization, urbanization, emerging welfare societies, dismantling of the rural areas, and professionalization of all walks of life. The impending death of the folk churches has been pronounced now and then. Still they exist, changing their roles in society, sometimes adapting to new situations, sometimes resisting new modes of living. Much thought was given to their national identity in the twentieth century.

The churches played a role in the internationalization that took place during the twentieth century. The missionary movement that began in the 1850s birthed many Scandinavian missionary agencies, some of them part of the church, others independent. The Finnish Missionary Society was, from 1870 on, very influential in Ovamboland in northern Namibia; the Norwegian Missionary Society (1842) operated in several countries, particularly Madagascar; the Danish Missionary Society (1821) was in Arcot and Jeypore in India; the Church of Sweden Mission (1874) had a presence particularly in Zimbabwe. These agencies operated in many more countries. There were scores of other missionary societies, but these were the ones closest to their folk churches. They were both voluntary associations and part of the official church. Through this north-south exchange the missionaries opened the eyes of the folk churches to the international world.

The ecumenical movement belongs to the twentieth century. Its aim was to bring the churches together after the split of confessionalism in the previous centuries. The issues of social ethics were stressed in a new way, particularly justice and peace. In several ways ecumenism has become part of all the Nordic folk churches. A hero in this aspect is Archbishop Nathan Söderblom (1866-1931), Uppsala. He summoned the churches to Stockholm in 1925 for a conference of life and work. His aim was to make the churches into peacemakers. Himself a researcher and lecturer in France, Germany, and England, he wanted these three Christian countries to reconcile and make peace. This conference was a landmark in the founding of the World Council of Churches.

In the academic disciplines the differences between the Nordic countries are often stressed. A typical remark about the four major churches is: "The Church of Norway and its Christians, the Church of Finland and its awakened, the Church of Denmark and its congregations, the Church of Sweden and its Swedish Church." To an outsider the similarities between the Nordic countries are more striking than the differences. In this book also the authors will stress the religious and cultural similarities between the Nordic countries and churches more than the differences. In the twentieth century the Nordic countries were challenged by Soviet Communism from the east and German National Socialism from the south. As democracies, they managed to stay clear from both, but in World War II they were drawn into the turmoil in different ways. For the churches it was easier to fight Communism, as it saw religion as an enemy. Most theologians were theologically and intellectually influenced by the German school of thought. It was harder for them to know how to meet the new order proclaimed by Hitler. The following chapters will show how this was done.

2. The Evangelical Lutheran Church in Denmark, 1940-2000

PETER LODBERG

In the Danish Constitution from 1849 and confirmed in 1953, the Evangelical Lutheran Church in Denmark is defined as the Danish folk church, and the Danish state is obliged to support it. The term "folk church" defines a church structure and a Lutheran ecclesiology that lies between state church and free church. To be a folk church means to have elements that are normally identified as important to either the state church or the free church. The concept and practice that keeps the state church and the free church together and gives the sole identity to the folk church is "voluntarism."

Before 1849, people were obliged to be members of the Evangelical Lutheran Church. In the new constitution the principle of freedom of religion was introduced, and membership in the church became a personal and voluntary matter. But it is important to understand that at the same time equality of religion was not introduced. The Evangelical Lutheran Church had — and still has — a privileged status. It is the only church that must be supported by the state. We recognize a double principle: freedom of religion, and the state-supported Evangelical Lutheran Church that is basic to Danish society even today.

The term "folk church" grew out of the democratic and popular movement in the middle of the nineteenth century. Behind the word "folk," as in "folk school," "folk university," "folk party," and "folk library," is the understanding of equality among people, who are created in the image of God. This ideal of relationship is the organizing principle in the different institutions that are established from below, i.e., organized by the people themselves.

During the German occupation of Denmark from April 9, 1940, to May 4, 1945, the Evangelical Lutheran Church played an important national role as a rallying point for many Danes. The war strengthened its identity as a folk church and as a national church. It gave new importance to an old figure called Lutheran Protestantism and nationhood, which has been an important element in church- and nation-building in Europe since the Reformation. The bishops, most clergy, and most congregations supported the Danish government and its policy of collaboration with the German occupiers. The idea was to save as much as possible of Danish society and welfare from devastation. Only in the autumn of 1943 did the situation change dramatically. The government resigned, and small resistance groups began to operate in the bigger cities. Kaj Munk, a very well known clergyman and writer, attacked the Germans forcefully and formulated a Christian-national protest, which was shared by most Danes. Munk was killed by the Germans in 1944 and became a national hero and symbol of Danish resistance.

After World War II, a leading Danish church historian, Hal Koch, maintained that life after the "Five Dark Years" continued "as if nothing had happened." He referred to the fact that Danish society was very intact. The old politicians, who collaborated with the Germans during the war, were reelected. At the same time, the public life and the private sector began to work as before 1940. Only in the area of ecumenism did the situation change a little bit.

Prior to World War II several leading figures in the folk church had close contacts with the emerging ecumenical movement. Among others, the bishop of Copenhagen, Hans Fuglsang-Damgaard, was very active in the establishment of the World Council of Churches (WCC). During the war he had close contacts with the Confessional Church in Germany and Dietrich Bonhoeffer. As a bishop he supported pastors and laypeople who took part in the resistance movement. In October 1943 he was one of the initiators of an open letter that protested the persecution of the Jews in Denmark and he helped some of them escape to Sweden. After the war he supported the establishment of a church-based refugee service to German refugees in Denmark, despite hard criticism from many Danes, who had forgotten all about the politics of collaboration during the war and now wanted revenge. Fuglsang-Damgaard considered the ecumenical movement an important player in the process of reconciliation with a war-torn Germany. It was evident to him that the folk church should be a founding member of the Lutheran World Federation (LWF) in 1947, the WCC in 1948, and the Conference of European Churches (CEC) in 1959. His contacts and experiences during the war helped to open the folk church to Christian churches in Europe and beyond.

Ecumenism was the folk church's postwar response to the process of internationalization that soon took the form of the Cold War, which lasted from 1946/47 to 1989/90. During the Cold War, close contacts were established between congregations in Eastern Europe and committed pastors and individuals in Denmark. In many cases Danchurchaid was an important bridge builder for personal contacts to Lutheran minority churches on the other side of the Iron Curtain. At the same time, Danchurchaid became more and more involved in humanitarian relief work and development aid in Africa, Asia, Latin America, and the Middle East. Danchurchaid became more global and ecumenical at the same time.

As did most Danes, Danchurchaid followed the official national line on the policy and practice toward churches and peoples in Eastern Europe. The idea was to collaborate and support local congregations as much as possible in accordance with the rules of the local authorities. Governments were not criticized for their policy toward the churches, but they were informed about the cooperation. The purpose was to create a free space for the local congregations to worship, educate, and live a Christian life in atheistic societies. This was in line with official Danish policy, which wanted to maintain the status quo and serve Danish interests of security and stability as a contribution to the American policy of containment toward the Eastern bloc.

The establishment of the Danish welfare state after World War II was the response to the Cold War and the challenges coming from Com-

During the Cold War, church leaders from the Nordic countries were meeting with representatives from the German Democratic Republic. Since they were not allowed to meet in Denmark, they gathered on a ship on international waters outside Aarhus, Denmark. Here, Danish Minister for Church Affairs Bodil Koch and colleagues sail to the conference ship anchored outside the territorial waters of Denmark.   Photo: WCC.

Bodil Koch, Danish Minister for Church Affairs, prepares to sail for a meeting of Nordic and East German church leaders.   Photo: WCC.

munist ideology and practice. Economic prosperity and social stability were important to the majority of the political parties. The Social Democratic Party (the Labour Party) played an especially important role in the political process toward the welfare state. It established a good relationship with the labor unions and challenged the presence of Communist unions among the labor force. The Social Democrats positioned themselves as a broad party with appeal to all sectors of society and had a leading role in most governments during the Cold War.

This party played a major role in relation to the folk church as well. Already in 1937 it had changed its policy of separation between state and folk church. It understood itself as the protector of the folk church as the people's church vis-à-vis any attempt by bishops, clergy, or certain interest groups to control or lead the church. Initiatives to change structure or to propose new developments in the folk church became a matter for the Parliament (the Folketing), and especially the ministers of church affairs and the civil servants in that ministry. This provided stability, and the folk church was included in the development of the welfare state as an institution that should guarantee coherence, meaning, and inclusiveness in a society that was changing dramatically. Thus, even though they had wanted a separation of state and church, the Social Democratic Party became a leading force in integrating the folk church into the new welfare state, and the religious service of the folk church was regarded as an important aspect of the state. This, of course, had serious consequences for the theological self-understanding of the folk church. The establishment of the welfare state challenged the theologians and the folk church to rethink its own ecclesiology and to formulate a new relationship between state and church. This paved the way for the Grundtvigian movement, which became the theological movement of the welfare state.

The Grundtvigian movement goes back to N. F. S. Grundtvig (1783-1872). He was a leading theologian, hymn writer, and politician in the national movement in the nineteenth century. During World War II Hal Koch reintroduced his importance to Danish identity through a series of lectures at the University of Copenhagen. Koch inspired a number of young theologians who played an important role in the folk church and on the theological faculties in Copenhagen and Aarhus. Among the most influential of the new theologians was P. G. Lindhardt, professor of church history at Aarhus. He became the theologian of the welfare state. His basic argument was that the Lutheran church would have to concentrate on worship, church rites, and youth education in confirmation classes. The folk church should have no say in political and public matters. In accordance with his ecclesiology, mission and *diaconia* should not be a matter for the official church structure. That should be left to voluntary church organizations outside the official structure. Lindhardt's understanding of faith was very individualistic. He believed that nobody should speak on behalf of the folk church in national or international forums, because this would patronize the individual and violate the Lutheran understanding of justification by faith alone.

Lindhardt regarded the welfare state and secularization of society as a positive challenge to the folk church to reconsider its Lutheran history and heritage. Secularization helped the folk church to regain the individuality of faith and to concentrate on worship and preaching as the only important aspects of Lutheran theology. He introduced a dualistic understanding of Luther's teaching of the two regiments both to argue for the separation of state and folk church and to de facto integrate the folk church into the welfare state.

Seen in the long historical perspective, Lindhardt and his many followers helped to formulate anew the identity between state, church, nation, and people that has been an important aspect in Danish society since the Reformation. From 1536 to 1849 the identity was made on the basis of absolutism; from 1849 to 1945 it was formulated on the basis of building a democratic and pluralistic nation-state; and after 1945 the welfare state has taken the role of the nation-state as the most important identity maker in Danish society. In all three periods the Lutheran church has played an important role: in the first period as state church, in the second period as a national folk church, and in the third as confessional welfare church.

Through most of the postwar period the Grundtvigian movement was challenged by the Inner Mission and church organizations inspired by the pietistic movement. They argued for a broader ecclesiology, where the official church would accept its responsibility for ecumenism, mission, and *diaconia*. These organizations had the experience of cooperation on a national basis in democratic structures, and they did not share the anxiety of the Grundtvigian movement for an independent church structure with a church assembly to speak for the folk church and take common initiatives. In 1954 the Council of Inter-Church Relationship was established as the focal point for cooperation between the folk church and the WCC, the LWF, and the CEC. In 1989 the structure was elaborated, and councils for interchurch relations were established in all dioceses in Denmark. This has created a new atmosphere of cooperation in the folk church, which has been helped by a common analysis by the different groups of the future challenges.

An important milestone has been a common analysis of the effect of secularization on the Danish youth. Efforts are now being made to establish Christian education by the folk church itself. This is a major change in policy and self-understanding. Earlier, the responsibility of Christian education was placed in the folk school and on the parents. Since 1975 the folk school has not been permitted to teach Christianity according to the tradition and teaching of the folk church. The result is a serious lack of the most basic knowledge in the Christian faith. This is considered a major challenge to the folk church in a more multicultural society and shows that the former identity between folk, nation, state, and church is very fragile, if it exists at all. The result is a stronger ecclesiological identity of the folk church and a willingness to take independent initiatives as a folk church in the Danish society.

As part of the welfare state, the folk church has benefited from the stability and economic growth in Danish society while at the same time helping the welfare state to succeed. The church membership fee is called the church tax and is collected through the state tax system. At the same time, the state pays the salaries of the bishops and supports the restoration work of some of the big churches that are considered national buildings. The folk church pays for and takes care of the registration of all Danes irrespective of church affiliation or religion. In many places the graveyards are also taken care of by the local church.

It is still unclear who benefits most from the present structure — the state or the folk church. Some will argue that the state is supported by the folk church — and not the other way around — because the expenses of the folk church for public registration and the running of the graveyards exceed the income from the state. The basic argument is that it is bad business for the state to separate from the folk church, because it will be too expensive for the state.

As is clear from this brief overview of some aspects of the relationship between the state and the folk church, the discussion has come up again after some years of silence. Basically, it is a discussion about the future relationship between nation, state, people, and church in a multicultural and multireligious society. All groups in the folk church want to maintain that relationship, but they disagree about the tools to secure the status quo under new circumstances. One group wants more freedom and independence of the folk church in order to respond actively to the new challenges to evangelization and mission, while another group wants the status quo, because it regards the present structure and work of the folk church as sufficient and in accordance with Lutheran teaching. What is new is that these two groups are cutting across the old divide between the Grundtvigian and pietistic movements.

Today the folk church consists of approximately 4.5 million people. This means that approximately 86 percent of the Danish population belongs to the folk church. Around 80 percent of all children are baptized into the Lutheran folk church; 80 percent of all youth take part in the confirmation classes; 53 percent of all marriages take place in the folk church; and 93 percent of the dead are buried by the folk church. When it comes to actual churchgoing, the numbers are very low. On a regular Sunday 1.3 percent of the population attends church services; about 3.9 percent of church members attend at least once a month. This paints a picture that could be called "belonging without participating." This picture has been stable for a number of years and is characteristic of the situation of the folk church today. Except for the number of funerals, there has been a slow but steady decline in all numbers in the period between 1940 and 2000. If this continues, the days of the folk church are numbered. According to the common understanding, the folk church can only maintain its status as a church supported by the state as formulated in the constitution as long as more than 50 percent of the population belongs to the Lutheran church. Thus, it is the people who decide if they want the Lutheran church in Denmark to be a folk church in the present meaning of the word. Only the future will tell if the folk church will survive. This should be possible, because the ability of the Lutheran church in Denmark to adjust to new situations is remarkable.

3. Finnish Christianity since 1940

Aila Lauha

Adjusting to Life after the War

At the end of World War II, about 96 percent of the Finnish population, at that time about 4 million in all, belonged to the Evangelical Lutheran Church. Although the country had had freedom of religion since 1923, the Orthodox Church was the only other major religion.

Beginning in the nineteenth century, when Finland was still under Russian rule, the Lutheran church strove to be a Finnish church, a nationally significant institution, a folk church. This role became particularly important when Finland won its independence from Russia in 1917. The leaders of the church understood it as an institution that worked with the people to offer guidance and consolation. The church was also a national force that took part in building the young nation. It taught that the fatherland was a gift from God: It was every Christian's duty to cherish this gift.

Finland was attacked by the Soviet army in November 1939. The short Winter War was over in March 1940, with heavy casualties. The war between Finland and the Soviet Union continued in the years 1941-44, also ending in great losses. During the last years of this war Finland was allied with Germany. Finland entered this alliance for military reasons, to get weapons for their own Soviet front, without cherishing any particular sympathy toward Hitler's regime. Nevertheless, the Finns in general, and the Lutheran church and its leadership in particular, did not react against the alliance. Firstly, there was a deep affinity between German and Finnish Lutheranism, based on manifold cultural and spiritual influences communicated from Germany to Finland over many centuries. Secondly, the Germans had given military aid to the "white" Finnish government during the civil war in 1918. At that time the church mainly supported the bourgeois and nonsocialistic "white" side. Therefore, the German military aid deepened the traditional confidence of the clergy in the Germans. At the end of the Second World War this confidence was given a severe shock: As the information about the Holocaust spread to Finland at the end of the war and especially after it, the atmosphere in the church was confused and depressed.

Finland itself did not experience persecutions. The Jewish men living in Finland were like other Finnish men on the front fighting against the Soviets, and even a camp synagogue was established for their use — to the great amazement of their German fellow fighters. Nevertheless, eight Jewish refugees were turned out from Finland on German orders and almost all of them died in the concentration camps. Among the Soviet war prisoners there were also Jewish men. It has recently been found out that several of them were sent to Germany through Finland.

Although the Finnish people and the Lutheran Church of Finland did not feel reason to share the shame and war guilt of the Germans, the alliance with Hitler's Germany was after the war a burden even in Nordic church relations. Especially Bishop Eivind Berggrav of Norway criticized the Finns and even the Finnish church leaders heavily for German sympathies.

During the war the church identified itself with the ordinary Finnish people who suffered on the front or at home, with the result that the position of the church in the lives of people was strengthened. After the war many European churches anticipated a general revival of religiosity. In Finland and in other Nordic countries the church worked to support the religious awakening of its people. The priests blended religious teachings with nationalism in their sermons, teaching that Christian values and cooperation with other Western churches would support the small Finnish nation in future times of need.

The war had underlined the dangers of extreme nationalism. Despite critical self-reflection by some clergymen, strong patriotism remained a typical feature in the Lutheran church. This outlook was transferred to the next generations as well. The anticommunist and anti-Soviet tendency also stayed with the church, even though it was expressed less explicitly than before the war. It is apparent that people's fear of a possible Soviet occupation and the uncertain political situation of Finland after World War II lent support to the Lutheran church, seen by many as a stable institution with strong Finnish values.

Moderate Reforms and New Tendencies

After the war the church responded to the rapid industrialization and urbanization of the country by developing new forms of social work. The church offered counseling to families, worked with industrial workers, alleviated the distress of the working poor, and developed its programs at hospitals. The church also looked for ways to refashion its image as a conservative and right-wing institution by engaging in a dialogue with the political left.

Even after the war and up until the early 1960s, the influence of the church still reached the private person very much in regard to his values, morals, and worldviews. Since the eighteenth century, pietistic movements have played a prominent role in Finnish religious culture. Up to at least the 1960s a good part of the Finnish clergy was influenced by pietism and its emphasis on individual piety. Although traditional pietistic revivalism lost some of its foothold in Finnish religious culture after the war, the new kinds of Anglo-American charismatic movements attracted people to mass meetings. During these meetings many participants, especially younger ones, experienced emotionally charged religious awakenings.

Newer forms of pietism left their mark in the Lutheran church, but such groups kept their distance from the institutional church, especially from the 1950s onward. One of the chief reasons for these groups' reservations concerning the Lutheran church was its perceived liberal stance toward moral and theological questions.

Some significant administrative changes were introduced to the church during the 1940s. Since 1869 the church has had its own General Church Assembly, responsible for ecclesiastical legislation and internal guidelines and reforms. This was complemented in the 1940s by two new administrative units, the Administrative Council (Kirkkohallitus) and the Expanded Meeting of the Bishops. In spite of these reforms, the president and the secular government of the country continued at the top of the ecclesiastical administration, thus exercising influence over nominations of bishops and other decision making. The Lutheran church has enjoyed considerable independence, but it has still formally remained a state church.

Until the late 1980s the church leaders and clergy were all men. Women were able to hold ecclesiastical offices either as deacons or as church musicians, and some urban parishes employed women with theological education for specific parish functions. The profession of parish organist was opened to women in 1963. At the same time, the question of women's ordination was brought up, with the result that the church established specially designed, but still limited, positions in the parishes for women with degrees in theology. When the Lutheran Church of Finland finally accepted women's ordination in 1988, it was the last Scandinavian Lutheran church to do so.

Contacts between Scandinavian churches and with Lutheran churches elsewhere in the world were important to Finland well before World War II. After the war these contacts among Lutherans, as well as ecumenical dialogue with other Christian denominations, became increasingly important for the Lutheran Church of Finland. During the immediate postwar years, Finland's church received donations from abroad, which significantly helped it rebuild. Membership in the World Council of Churches and the Lutheran World Federation helped Finnish theologians and clergy strengthen their ties with Western Christian churches.

Finland's small but culturally significant Greek Orthodox minority provided Finns an opportunity for a constant ecumenical exchange between Eastern and Western Christianities. During the immediate postwar years, about 1.8 percent of Finns belonged to the Greek Orthodox

In Finland, up to 90 percent of each age group still takes part in confirmation schools. This is greater than the percentage of Finns who belong to the Lutheran church.

Church weddings are still very popular in Finland.

Female pastors have been ordained in the Lutheran Church of Finland since 1988.

In 1974, Archbishop Martti Simojoki was awarded a high Swedish decoration by the King of Sweden. Here, Archbishop Olof Sundby, left, congratulates his colleague.

On the last day of the summer revival festival of 2004, more than twenty-five thousand people took part.

Old and young take part in summer revival festivals of the pietist movement called The Awakened (*Herättäjäjuhlat*). Standing on the left is Matti
Sihvonen, former Bishop of Kuopio.

Church, but from the 1950s onward this number dropped to about 1.5 percent. In 1923 the Greek Orthodox Church of Finland withdrew from the patriarchate of Moscow and joined the Ecumenical Patriarchate of Constantinople as an autonomous church. Simultaneously the church was officially granted status as a state church that shared the same privileges as the Evangelical Lutheran Church.

The ecumenical organization of Finland was established in 1917 and is today called the Finnish Ecumenical Council. It has brought together not only Lutherans and Orthodox Christians but also members of most other Protestant minority denominations of Finland. The Roman Catholic Church of Finland, which was reestablished in 1929 after being banned at the time of the Reformation, has today about eight thousand members. It became a member of the Finnish Ecumenical Council in the 1950s. Although the ecumenical dialogue in Finland remained for quite some time in the hands of a small group of enthusiastic clergymen and laypeople, as it did in Norway, it slowly succeeded in fostering tolerance and mutual understanding between all Christian denominations in Finland.

The Church in Finland — between East and West

Finland's political realities differed from those of the other Scandinavian countries. Finland suffered devastating losses during the Second World War and lost about 12 percent of its land and 13 percent of its national wealth to the Soviet Union. Some 2.5 percent of its inhabitants died from war-related causes, and more than 400,000 had to be evacuated from eastern Finland to other parts of the country. The other Scandinavian countries did not experience similar human and material losses. Finland's geopolitical circumstances and its heavy war debt to the Soviet Union put it in danger of losing its political independence and of being brought under Soviet dominion in the 1950s when the Soviet Union strengthened its hold over other European countries bordering it.

Finland managed to retain its independence and successfully balanced itself between the East and the West during the years of the Cold War. Thus Finland's church avoided the fate of Eastern European churches, which had to defend their right to exist. Finland's own political left kept fairly good relations with the church. In 1946 the Social Democratic Party removed from its agenda the demand for the separation of the church and the state.

The church worked to strengthen its relations with the left and looked for new ways to draw closer to the working class. This was particularly difficult to accomplish in regard to groups on the far left, including members of the Communist Party. These groups worked not only to separate the church and the state, but also to diminish the role of religion in Finnish society. They were particularly critical of religious education in the schools and strove to replace it with the teaching of secular ethics. Despite heavy political debate and extensive committee work, the denominational teaching of religion was kept at public schools, although the number of lessons was slightly reduced.

After World War II the church benefited from its strong and open-minded bishops who were ready to look for new directions without compromising the church's own good. Bishops had intellectual and spiritual influence on Finnish politicians, but they typically stayed away from politics. During his long time as a president, Urho Kekkonen (1956-81) respected the church and people's religious beliefs. (See the biographical sketch of Kekkonen in chapter 9.) At the time of elections politicians took care not to offend people's religious values.

Even though the Communist Party voiced strong criticism of the church, Finland did not experience a mass movement away from the church. Even most of the Communists held on to their church membership, allowing their children to be baptized and take part in the religious education in schools and in the church. The Lutheran church did, however, lose some of its membership base during the second half of the twentieth century. In 1960 about 92 percent of Finns belonged to the church, but that number had dropped to about 87 percent by 1990. In 2004 the Finnish population was about 5.1 million, of which about 85 percent were members of the Lutheran church.

Church and Radicalism

During the 1960s radical leftist movements and liberal worldviews spread to Finland. These movements challenged traditional religious values and ethical codes. Especially the press and young intelligentsia criticized the Christian worldview as unscientific and nonrational. Some worked, without success, to remove religious education from the school curriculum. The young people drew parallels between the church and other conservative institutions, such as the army. They tried to distance themselves from the church's teachings concerning sexual morality and its puritan values.

University students focused on the problems they saw in the church's socioethical message and the church's role in the Third World. The students argued that Christian faith was part of the capitalistic system. According to them, the Christian mission promoted Western values that furthered the exploitation of Third World countries and destroyed old cultures. Some critics argued that universal justice was possible only through a profound social change in the developed world. This criticism gained some support even among the church's own youth groups.

During the most intense years of Communist radicalism in the 1970s, supporters of the Lutheran church feared it would lose its position as a folk church. Bishops engaged in the dialogue by publishing pamphlets and participating in panels that addressed international and socioeconomic questions. Archbishops Martti Simojoki (1964-78) and Mikko Juva (1978-82) made significant contributions to discussions concerning the church's social responsibilities and the need for church reform. (See the biographical sketch of Simojoki in chapter 9.) They acted as the church's voice in society, creating a practice that was to be emulated by future archbishops.

New Initiatives and Modernization of the Church

Since the middle of the 1960s the Lutheran Church of Finland has changed in many significant respects. The liturgical life went through a considerable reform. The new liturgical rite was established in 1968, and in the 1990s several new liturgical reforms, which combined elements from the Lutheran heritage and other church traditions, were introduced to establish liturgical practices appropriate to modern times and people. A new hymnal was put into use in 1986, and the new Finnish translation of the Bible was introduced in 1992. Church legislation was reformed in 1994. A new catechism interpreting the main contents of Evangelical Lutheran belief for a modern reader was delivered to all Finnish homes in 2000.

In debates concerning religion, the focus moved away from socioethical questions toward sexual ethics and interpretations of the Bible. Although the church took a notably cautious and traditional stance on questions concerning same-sex marriage and homosexuality, some conservative groups reacted against the church and created their own pressure groups within it.

The most debated question inside the church was women's ordination. Women have been ordained as priests since 1988, but the practice still creates controversy. The historical-critical interpretation of the Bible created some heated debates.

Higher theological education in Finland is offered at universities. There are no separate theological seminaries, although their formation has been brought up at times. The universities of Helsinki and Joensuu, as well as the Swedish-speaking Åbo Akademi in Turku, offer theological education at both undergraduate and graduate levels. The Department of Theology at the University of Joensuu specializes in both Lutheran and Orthodox theologies.

Did the Church Experience Its Form of "Finlandization"?

The Cold War had a strong impact on Finland's foreign policy, especially at times of international conflicts. The church followed political developments closely and avoided statements they feared could hurt the country's national interests.

Since the collapse of the Soviet Union in 1991, the church's role dur-

ing the Cold War years has come under heated discussion. It has been debated whether the church experienced its own form of "Finlandization"
(Finlandizierung), whether it was too cautious toward the Soviet Union.

It is evident that especially during the 1960s and 1970s Finland was
careful not to criticize the Soviet Union and its suppression of religious
freedom. In part, this strategic silence was motivated by fear for Finland's future, but the church also feared that public statements could
worsen the plight of Christians living behind the Iron Curtain.

Despite the church's silence concerning the Soviet Union's antireli-
gious politics, the clergy and the practicing members of the church did
not sympathize with the Soviet politics. The bitter memories of the war
and the ideological drift between Soviet atheism and Christian faith
strengthened the resentment the Finnish church felt toward the Soviet
Union. The Communist newspapers in Finland even labeled the church
anti-Soviet, although the church did not make open comments against
the Soviet Union.

At the Beginning of a New Millennium

At the beginning of the millennium Finland is an increasingly multicultural society. Immigration from African countries and the Balkans has
brought Finland a fairly large and active Muslim population. In 2003 a
new law concerning religious freedom was passed, guaranteeing all religious groups a right to practice their faiths and receive religious education in their own faith at schools.

Baptism, confirmation, and religious rites at burials have continued
to be popular among Finns, and big church weddings have again become fashionable. Nevertheless, only 2 percent of Finns participate frequently in Sunday mass. In smaller cities the attendance is slightly
higher. The church has looked for new ways to serve its members. It offers day care, parenting classes, clubs for single people, support groups
for recovering alcoholics, and other forms of counseling and social care.
The so-called Thomas Masses, named after doubting Thomas, which
combine gospel music, new forms of prayer, and a strong sense of com-

munity, have reached young and educated members of the church in the bigger towns. Charismatic movements have continued to attract people.

The church plays an important role at the time of both private and collective celebrations. It brings a sense of security and continuity to people's lives. For many people the value of religion becomes evident at times of personal and social crises. During the recession of the 1990s the church looked for new ways to support people during economic difficulties. It organized soup kitchens, offered help with debt consolidation, and spoke strongly for social equality. The church's strident efforts to offer relief for the unemployed and other people in need clearly strengthened its position as an ideological force within the country. The bishops, especially the long-term and widely respected archbishop John Vikstöm (1982-98) and his solid and plainspoken successor Jukka Paarma (elected in 1999), have been frequently seen in the media to address contemporary ethical and social problems.

The Lutheran church's profile and image have gone through profound changes during the last decades of the twentieth century. The church is still a decisively national, Finnish, institution. At the same time, it has taken an active interest in international and ecumenical exchange. The Lutheran Church of Finland is still fairly traditional in its teachings concerning dogmatic aspects of faith, but its understanding concerning sexual ethics and marriage has broadened. As a folk church it shelters many types of religious groups and a wide variety of religious beliefs. The church believes that the celebration of plurality is one of the best ways for it to prosper in the future.

4. The Church of Norway since World War II

GUNNAR HEIENE

The Second World War (1939-45) created a political and military situation that made the differences between the Nordic countries and folk churches more visible than ever. The Nordic countries experienced the war from quite different perspectives. Finland had its unique experiences through the attack from the Soviet Union in 1939, while Denmark and Norway were occupied by Germany on April 9, 1940. Iceland kept close contact with United States during the war, while Sweden maintained strict neutrality.

For Norway the experiences from April 1940 to May 1945 were quite determinative for the years and decades afterward. The attack on Oslo and other major cities in the morning of April 9 was a shocking experience for the Norwegian people, who had hoped to keep neutral. Lots of people tried to escape to safer places, and the situation was rather chaotic. Politicians and other leading persons were also confused and looked for ways of handling the situation that would save lives, while many Norwegians wanted to risk their lives fighting against the German troops.

One of the most profiled Norwegian leaders in this period was Bishop Eivind Berggrav, in the diocese of Oslo. (See the biographical sketch of Berggrav in chapter 9.) He played a very active part in the political discussions among the leadership in the first weeks of the occupation, and was a member of the so-called Administration Council established to normalize the situation. Some of his actions were misused by German propaganda and misunderstood among the Allies, but no doubt Berggrav helped to give the church an important role as a leading institution in a time of severe crisis.

The role of the Norwegian church became even more important in the following years, especially after the formation of Kristent Samråd (The Joint Christian Council) in September 1940, where the bishops and representatives for different lay Christian movements united in a common action to protect the integrity of the church and to protest against unethical acts from the Nazi government.

The most dramatic events in the church-state relations during the occupation took place in April 1942, when a group of church leaders within Kristent Samråd wrote a confessional declaration, called *Kirkens Grunn* (The foundation of the church). In deepest secrecy the declaration was distributed to most of the Norwegian congregations, and on Easter Day it was read in the churches. Most of the pastors (93 percent) broke their relationship with the state and declared, according to *Kirkens Grunn*, that they would uphold their position as leaders of the congregations, within the framework of a free Norwegian Lutheran church. The attempts from the Nazi authorities to establish an "official" church led by pastors and "bishops" who were loyal to the state was a failure. In most parts of the country the Nazi church had very limited support.

Bishop Berggrav was arrested a few days after the dramatic events on Easter 1942. He spent the last three years of the occupation as a prisoner in his own cabin outside Oslo, and although he managed to be in contact with other leaders both within the church and within the resistance movement, the leadership had to be given to other church leaders. A provisional church leadership (Den Midlertidige Kirkeledelse) was established, with people like Professor Ole Hallesby from the Inner Mission and Menighetsfakultetet (The Lutheran School of Theology), and Ludvig Hope, leader of a low-church organization (Kinamisjonsforbundet), as important members.

The cooperation between bishops and church leaders from different positions within the Church of Norway was an important and new experience within the church, which had for decades been characterized by severe disagreement and controversies between "conservatives" and "liberals." The support from churches in the free world also helped to create a better ecumenical climate, and after the war Berggrav and other Norwegian church leaders increased their efforts to integrate the Church of Norway into the new ecumenical organizations.

Although the end of the war in May 1945 led to a spontaneous outbreak of celebration in Norway, it soon became clear that peace meant new challenges that had to be solved. One main problem was how to deal with those who had supported the Norwegian Nazi Party (Nasjonal Samling), led by Vidkun Quisling. Some of the leading members of the party committed suicide, while others, like Quisling himself, were imprisoned. Not only the leaders but also ordinary party members were arrested, and in July 1945, 14,000 people were imprisoned for supporting the Nazi Party. A total of 46,000 Norwegian Nazi members were punished, 25 of whom (including Quisling) suffered the death penalty. The traitors (*landssvikere*) and their families protested the many cases against them, and the wounds created by the strong antagonism between the two groups within the Norwegian population during the war have been painful in the decades after the war. Bishop Berggrav provoked many Norwegian patriots with a clear statement against the death penalty. The bishops were called "silk bishops" by the press, and were accused of being too "soft" against the traitors. On the other hand, Berggrav also provoked the Nazi members and their families, claiming that all members of the party had a personal guilt and deserved punishment regardless of which acts they had been involved in during wartime.

The northern part of Norway suffered severely during the last year of the war, especially since the German troops withdrew in that direction to escape the Russian soldiers, who were received as liberators in this area. In 1947, Norway agreed to join the so-called Marshall Plan, and although many politicians feared that her neutrality could be threatened, it became more and more obvious that Norway needed help from abroad to recover materially and financially after the war.

Politically, the first years after the war were characterized by common efforts to overcome the problems created by the war, and the first election showed increased support for the Social Democrats and the

Communists. The Christian Democratic Party (Kristelig Folkeparti) also strengthened its position in Parliament. This led to a discussion among church leaders about the relationship between Christianity and politics. Should Christian believers gather in a specific Christian party, or should they vote according to their political ideas and support the different political parties from right to left?

Of course, the war also created specific problems for the church and the congregations. Although the Nazi pastors were only a small minority, the church had to react, and these pastors were denied access to positions in the church. In June 1945 the church presented a list of seventy pastors who had been members of the National Socialist Party. It was not until 1955 that these pastors were given the opportunity to serve within the church, and only a few of them came back as pastors.

Also problematic for the church after the war were the challenges from a secularized culture. It soon became clear that the popular support for the church during the war could not last in peacetime. One specific problem was that the church faced competition from other institutions on economic matters. Many churches, especially in the north, were destroyed. Money from American Lutheran churches was welcomed in this situation. A more severe problem was the cultural and ideological changes that became more visible after the war, represented by a tendency toward secularization, pluralism, and a more marginal position for Christian faith. New initiatives were taken within the church to meet these challenges. Some pastors were given a special opportunity to work among the secularized people, especially in urban areas. In 1945, leading persons within the church established a Christian newspaper, *Vårt Land,* which was seen as part of the Christian cultural endeavor, and the same year an Institute for Christian Education (IKO) was established. Within the church the concept of a Norwegian "folk church" was still influential, and in the first years after the war there were still hopes for a closer relationship between church and people, based on the common experiences during the occupation. But it soon became clear that hopes for a new national Christian awakening were an illusion.

At the same time, there were also attempts at reforming the relationship between state and church. The church's aim in these attempts was to get more freedom than the old state church system had allowed. Of course, the church struggle against Nazism had shown that she needed freedom and that situations could arise where she had to take a clear stand against political decisions. In 1945 Berggrav published a pamphlet written during the war, *Kirkens ordning i Norge* (Church organization in Norway), where he proposed several reforms within the state church. The political parties agreed that a commission should be established to elaborate these issues, and from autumn 1945 Berggrav led such a group that worked with proposals that could give the church better conditions within the state church system. The commission published its proposals in 1948, but the debate in the following years, especially within Parliament, showed little enthusiasm for radical changes, and when the new church law was established in 1953, only minor improvements had taken place.

The main opponents of reforms in the church were politicians within the Labour Party, who feared that too much freedom for the church could destroy the folk church and lead to a situation where "the inner circle" of the congregations got too much power on behalf of the many "passive" church members. The party also feared that the conservative part of the church would get too much power and wanted to create possibilities for more "liberal" bishops.

In 1953, in the months before the final discussions on the new church legislation in Parliament, a theological controversy (described in chapter 8) increased the tensions within the church between the conservatives and the liberals. During the occupation there had been much cooperation between different groups within the church, but the discussions on eternal punishment between Professor Hallesby of Menighetsfakultetet and the liberal bishop of Hamar, Kristian Schjelderup, revealed that the old antagonism from the theological struggle in the first decades of the century still existed. In the following years the split between different theological groups within the church became even more visible, and new theological issues took over as "test cases": the issues of female pastors, of divorce and remarriage, and, in later years, of homosexuality. In 1961 the first female pastor in Norway, Ingrid Bjerkås, was ordained by Bishop

45

Schjelderup, and for many years the debate on this issue created much tension within the church. Four decades later, all the bishops and most of the pastors and theological professors welcomed female pastors. This shift of opinion illustrates a more general tendency of accommodation in Norwegian church life.

Also, considerable development in the field of ecumenism has taken place within the church. The ecumenical experiences during the war inspired Berggrav and other leaders to work for better ecumenical contacts, on a national as well as an international level. The church became a member of the new international and ecumenical organizations, the World Council of Churches and the Lutheran World Federation (and from 1959 the Conference of European Churches), but in the first decades ecumenical work was to a certain extent an elitist activity. Today it is integrated much deeper into the church, and the understanding and contact between different churches and denominations has improved a lot. On the national level the first steps were taken in 1950, when Berggrav invited free church leaders to form a "Contact Circle" for ecumenical work. A decisive step was taken when Norway's Christian Council was established in 1992. Although the increasing ecumenical involvement was criticized, especially by low-church pietistic groups, the climate has changed during the last decades. In 1970 the ecumenical work within the Church of Norway was reorganized and strengthened through its Council on Ecumenical and International Relations, which had been established in 1952. In the last three decades, the global perspective and the strong focus upon international solidarity have led to a change of attitude which has also had consequences for the ecumenical climate in Norway. In local congregations these changes have also been very visible through a strengthened ecumenical practice. The Norwegian church has joined the Porvoo Agreement with the Anglican Church, it has signed the Leuenberg Agreement, and it has also established a close relationship to the Methodist Church in Norway (Nådens fellesskap [The Fellowship of Grace]).

The global perspective has also changed the profile of the Christian relief organization in Norway (Kirkens Nødhjelp [Norwegian Church Aid]). This organization was established in 1947, and its aim was to help refugees and other suffering people in European countries after the war. But increasingly it has assumed global responsibility, and today is represented in many different countries in the Third World, in close cooperation with the governmental institutions for development and human rights.

On the national level, the relationship between state and church has been discussed several times since legislation was passed in 1953. From time to time church leaders have tried to get support for new reforms, and important changes have taken place. A leader in this reform process has been Andreas Aarflot, the former bishop of Oslo (1977-98). In 1984 the first official General Assembly (Kirkemøtet) took place, and the importance of this annual assembly has increased. But still, the relationship between state and church is debated, and it seems as if church leaders are more radical than the average population on this issue. Many people fear that the folk church will be threatened if the close ties between state and church disappear. The bishop of Oslo, Gunnar Stålsett, has strongly defended the concept of folk church and warned against too quick steps toward a schism between state and church.

Both on a national and an international level the church has developed a stronger social-ethical profile after the war. Again, the experiences from the church struggle against a totalitarian state have been important. After 1968 the social-ethical movement within the church became more permanent. The focus on environmental issues and global justice in the church parallels the political interest in such issues, as shown in Prime Minister Gro Harlem Brundtland's international engagement. (See the biographical sketch of Brundtland in chapter 9.) In other ethical issues the disagreement between the church and the politicians, especially the Labour Party, has been considerable. The abortion law caused a lot of debates in the 1970s and 1980s, and different strategies were identified in different parts of the church. Bishop Per Lønning chose a line of confrontation, resigning from his position, while a pastor in the north, Børre Knudsen, went even further, protesting very actively against the new law on abortion. Other church leaders have chosen a "softer" strategy, trying to influence attitudes toward abortion and to work for social improvements that could lead to a decrease in abortions.

The debates on issues like abortion and sexual ethics show that Norway has become a more pluralized and secularized country. Christianity no longer has a monopoly when it comes to ethical and religious discussions. Immigration from many countries, especially Muslim countries, has strengthened the tendency toward pluralism. But at the same time, it is possible to see signs of retraditionalization and resacralization. Religious issues have become more important in society, especially compared to the first decades after the war. For many years the number of baptisms decreased, but in the last few years there have been signs of an increase. This is an indication that the folk church is still a vital concept in a new millennium.

5. Church of Sweden, 1940-2000

Björn Ryman

Population

In the twentieth century Sweden was the largest country in Scandinavia both in area and population. Centrally located among the Scandinavian countries, it often had to take the lead. Sweden was the only country that managed to stay out of World War II. This led to envy from the other countries during and after the war.

Swedish population had increased to 9 million by the year 2000. This is due to immigration, particularly in the years since 1970, during which many political refugees have been given asylum. About 1 million people have entered from outside Sweden. At the same time, the Swedish population is aging. The number of people receiving pensions has reached one-third of the population. This is particularly true in rural areas, which witnessed a migration of young people to the urban areas. These plain facts about population affected the Swedish religious landscape immensely. Firstly, the most ardent adherents of the Church of Sweden live in the rural areas, and this diminishing and aging population should have the same traditional religious services in terms of a church, church services, parish boards, pastors in residence, and congregational activities. Secondly, most of those who moved to the cities for studies and employment lost contact with the church and became part of a secularized society. Thirdly, new churches established in Sweden were some of the oldest traditional churches from the Middle East as well as some of the newest charismatic congregations from the United States. To a national folk church, organized according to fixed territorial parishes and archaic church orders, this meant many challenges.

Politics

Sweden the Middle Way was the title of a book for an American audience in the 1930s. The welfare state took shape in several European countries. In Scandinavia the leading roles were played by Social Democratic labor parties. They remained democratic and kept the reformist tradition. Scandinavian countries were among the few democratically governed states in the 1930s. The Social Democratic prime minister launched the concept of the welfare state in 1928. He used the term *folkhemmet* — a home for the people — as a metaphor for the new nation to be built. The word "folk" was greatly misused by the Nazis in Germany. But the concept of folk was essential to the vision of the Social Democratic Party and activists within the church. It gave identity to both party and church.

Under Social Democratic hegemony there were endless debates and commissions on church-state relations and the ordination of women. These two issues were dominated by the politicians and not by theologians or church people.

Economics

The financial world crisis around 1930 also hit Scandinavia. One practice of the Social Democrats was to control financial flows nationally. National economics was applied by the Stockholm school — a Keynesian method launched in Sweden prior to Keynes and Franklin Roosevelt. Compromises and alliances were made with other parties and powerful corporate organizations. Labor and management agreed to cooperate instead of escalating labor conflicts. A corporate state emerged that was dominated by Social Democratic prime ministers and loyal institutions. The war years were not traumatic but were considered a parenthesis in the social and economic development. A coalition government ruled Sweden during the war years. The period 1948-73 can be considered golden years in Swedish economic history, with unlimited economic growth and a tremendous expansion of the public sector, taking as much as 57 percent of GNP. All Swedes gained from this enhancement of social benefits, new pension system, better education for all. This was "Sweden the middle way." The role of the church, however, was marginalized in this process. True, as a state church its income was kept at a steady level, paying salaries and pensions for clergy in 2,500 parishes, keeping up 4,000 church buildings, and constructing many new parish halls. As a matter of fact, 700 new churches were built in the new suburbs — the greatest number ever. The welfare and affluent society was also criticized for bringing about materialistic values, alienating the people from religion. This was a theme in sermons of the period.

Church Leadership

Archbishop Nathan Söderblom had been a charismatic leader and a personality of great international and ecumenical reputation. His strength as a social communicator convincing people about ideas was acknowledged by many. After his death in 1931 the liberal government unexpectedly appointed the professor of New Testament from the University of Lund, Erling Eidem, as his successor. Considered a humble and pious man, well versed in traditional theology but lacking experience in church leadership and ecumenism, his image was the opposite of Söderblom's. His patience was put to many tests during his eighteen years as archbishop. The most difficult for him was the development in Germany — a country he loved from his student days. Like many other theologians, medical doctors, and engineers, he considered German culture and German universities the ideal. Swedish leaders were as unprepared to meet the challenges from National Socialism as those in Germany itself. Eidem had around him a group of theologians who carried forward the ecumenical program of Söderblom both in Sweden and abroad. Together they managed to stay in active contact with the Confessing Church in Germany and members of the resistance group, Kreisau. Through the Swedish pastors in Berlin and Oslo, Eidem was well informed of the situation, and through them much was done to save people from the atrocities of the war. As a government official in a neutral country, however, the archbishop was not allowed to further his own peace initiatives. However, neither church nor state was proud of its accomplishments during the war, when all efforts were geared at keeping Sweden outside the war. More on this in the next chapter.

More of a Söderblom type of church leader was Manfred Björkquist (1884-1985), unofficial leader of the young church movement, founder of the Sigtuna foundation, and an initiator of many new church projects on a national scale. He and his Sigtuna became the rallying point for many activists, particularly students, who entered dialogue with the non-church world of socialists, authors, and intellectuals. Björkquist was appointed bishop in the newly created diocese of Stockholm in 1942.

The church leadership was both academically distinguished and highly respected by the people, and spoke with authority. The age of the strong bishops lasted until the 1960s, when there was a great shift in society. Few if any women could be among the leaders in the Church of Sweden at this time. A new age was in the making. The strong bishops of high academic standing and cultural conservatism, who spoke with authority, had to yield to democratically elected persons in dialogue with the people at large.

Church Politics

The two dominant issues facing the folk church were decided more by politicians in Parliament than by church councils and synods. They were whether women could be pastors and whether the state should be separated from the church. After many heated debates the first women pastors were ordained in 1960, the most well-known being Margit Sahlin,

Th.D. and Ph.D. While the exegetes of the theological faculties said no and most of the followers of the church revival movements as well as the high-church movement refused to accept women as their clergy, the church assembly stipulated a new church law in 1958. Those resisting were allowed a clause of conscience in not cooperating. The issue of gender equality weighed heavier on most Swedes than theological reasons. The issue for many years split the church and drained its life of much needed energy. By the millennium there were two women bishops, Christina Odenberg in Lund and Caroline Krook in Stockholm. Approximately one thousand women served as parish pastors — one-third of the clergy. A woman was also appointed secretary-general of the Church of Sweden when formal ties were eventually broken with the state in 2000.

Church and state never completely separated. The relationships became gradually different. An American could say there is no separation between church and state in Sweden. To some Swedes the changing relationship was a blow to their concept of a national folk church. Still, the royal family want to be members of the Evangelical Lutheran Church of Sweden. Most Swedes, 80 percent, want to be paying members, and their fees are still collected by the revenue authority, approximately 1 percent of annual income. The services of the church are asked for by most members. Eighty-seven percent are buried according to church rites. The church is also responsible for the whole funeral system. Around 71 percent of parents let their children be baptized, but confirmation of fifteen-year-olds had dropped to 50 percent by 2000. For how long can a folk church still be called a national folk church? The majority of the people still request her services and appreciate them, but a gradual decline is taking place.

Around 1900 the theology of the folk church developed. It was a religiously motivated theology in confrontation with that of the free churches. God's grace was extended to all people regardless of their religious decisions. Everybody within the parish territory was to feel included in the church. "The people of Sweden — a people of God" was a slogan of the young church movement from 1910 up to World War II. This was interpreted as a future-oriented vision of the church to be rather than a realistic description of the present-day church. Ideologically it was an affront against German Christians who misused the term "folk" as an expression of the Germanic folk as the chosen people of God. During World War II a well-known motto was "Sweden's line is the Christian line." There was much rallying around this theme. The churches were held in high esteem by the people at large during this time of crisis. An estimated 44 percent listened to the daily morning prayers and Sunday services, which were broadcast on the only national radio channel available. The height of the war years was a climax of the folk church in the twentieth century. Prospects looked favorable.

Alas, the *annus mirabilis* turned into the *annus horribilis*. The immediate postwar years were full of attacks on a church turned defensive. There were accusations of clergymen having been too favorable to Germany, some even expressing pro-Nazi sympathies. Mistakes had been made by church leadership. From the political left, whose strength culminated from 1945 to 1948, attacks against the official church were many. Lately Sweden has officially taken great pains to interpret its own actions in the Holocaust. The prime minister has been lauded for an information campaign on living history. There are only a few examples of rescue actions at the end of the war, Raoul Wallenberg in Budapest being the most outstanding, saving tens of thousands of doomed Jews. The churches are accused of having done too little. However, the ecumenical circles protested from 1933 on against Hitler's persecutions. Clergy stationed in Berlin and Vienna undertook heroic interventions to save Jews and bring them to Sweden. From Vienna three thousand children of Jewish origin were transported to freedom in other countries. Swedish clergy in Germany also assisted Count Folke Bernadotte in rescuing mainly Scandinavian prisoners in concentration camps. The lesson from the Holocaust and the ethnic cleansing was that the churches must take seriously the issue of human rights, regardless of confession, and not be afraid to intervene in what was considered the political realm.

On another level there was the debate on faith and scientific knowledge. The epicenter of this debate was the University of Uppsala. A professor of analytical philosophy, Ingemar Hedenius, conducted an intellectual crusade against Christian faith and believing theologians for evading the issue of philosophical and scientific truth. Through books and public debates, theologians and pastors were challenged to defend Christian faith philosophically and intellectually. According to his analysis, only rational, value-free arguments mattered, which could be held true or falsified. Human beings were rational, and society at large and education in particular should strive to be objective. Neutrality should be observed between different worldviews. In the eyes of public opinion Anders Nygren and other theologians lost the debate. (See the biographical sketch of Nygren in chapter 9.)

The role of Hedenius was immense in the academic world, but also in the political. Most of the Social Democratic reform proposals for the welfare state should be value-free, he contended. The control of the state church was no longer so important as the command over the schools. In the reforms for better education for all, the grip of the folk church over school morning prayers and confessional instruction on the subject of Christianity had to go. Although public opinion favored religious instruction in schools, a change was definitely on the way. The degree of secularization in Swedish society can be measured in the way the influence of the folk church on education was diminished throughout the century. Key words in this process were "democratic attitudes," "objectivity," "the student in focus," "free choice," and "pluralism." The monolithic world of the folk church had to go. Its norms were no longer the favored values.

The church had to be on the offensive to bring its own educational efforts up to date. A different nonauthoritarian pedagogical method was introduced in confirmation groups. Now it was the life experience of the fifteen-year-olds in the center and not the answers of the church. Groups for young children were started in every parish. The folk church now had to approach its members as any other free church.

Sweden also had its share of student revolts in 1968, the heyday of revolt. A peculiar incident was the hosting of the WCC General Assembly at Uppsala during the summer of 1968. Revolution was in the air when authoritarian bishops, esteemed professors, and skillful church organizers were brushed aside by young people with a burning desire for justice for the oppressed, equality for all. The Western world and its support for the American policy of dominance in particular was attacked. It was a shift of values in society and also in the churches. Ethics for the individual was replaced by ethics for society. Rigid anticommunism gave way to a spirit of cooperation with socialist countries and liberation movements with revolutionary goals. The list could go on. Some church historians have suggested that the revolution of thought in 1968 had a greater impact than the Protestant Reformation in the 1520s.

The folk church had to take the signals from 1968 seriously. Most evident were the international issues of justice and peace. This was not just a hobby of the academic elite. On the parish level there was an increase of involvement in Third World issues and matters of justice. Many debates were held about how the rich countries were to blame for the condition of the poor countries. Fund-raising for the church agencies for emergency and development aid was intensified during these years. The mission agencies also shifted emphasis from traditional missionary activities to a South-North exchange. The international perspective became a perspective of the local parish.

It is true that traditional Lutheran theology of the Lundensian sort lost ground. The high point for this church theology with a thought-through system for the whole church was 1942, when the leading theologians published *A Book on the Church*. It did not exert the expected influence. Here was a presentation of how a national church — a folk church — could justify its existence theologically. As we have seen, a new type of society was emerging with a new type of individualism not asking for guidelines from theological authorities. In this vacuum of classical theology, new branches developed with inspiration from other fields: sociology of religion, psychology of religion, studies of faith and ideologies instead of dogmatics. This attempt to make theology as respected as any other scientific discipline was a result of the philosophical debate in the 1950s. At the end of the century, inspiration came from liberation theology in Latin America, black theology from Africa, and greater gender awareness through feminist theology. This affected the education of the clergy, who before 1970 were educated in a more classical way by the universities of Uppsala and Lund. From now on theological education became more diversified and decentralized. The church organized the last year of education for the clergy as a practical year.

Church music is much favored in the folk church. The standard of

The Nordic royal families attend church services and other church events. Here, outside Uppsala Cathedral in Sweden, King Carl Gustaf is escorted by the dean, Tuulikki Koivunen Bylund, and Queen Silvia is escorted by the Archbishop, K. G. Hammar.   Photo: Jim Elfström, IKON.

An ecumenical service in Uppsala in 1993 included, from the left, Cardinal Cassidy and Archbishop Gunnar Weman of Uppsala, Patriarch Bartilimaios of Constantinople, and Archbishop John Vikström of Turku, Finland.

In 1989, the late Pope John Paul II was the first pope ever to visit the five Nordic countries. Here he greets Archbishop Bertil Werkström and his wife Britta in Uppsala.

Sewing associations meeting regularly in Swedish parishes have been the main supporters of missionary and diaconal work.   Photo: Jim Elfström, IKON.

A confirmation takes place in the medieval church of Vaksala, Sweden. The tradition of youth confirmation is about three hundred years old in the Nordic churches, but participation is diminishing, especially in Sweden.
Photo: Jim Elfström, IKON.

education is very high for the organists. Cathedral organists in Sweden rank very high artistically. At the same time, the big churches are the best concert halls for classical music like the *Passions* of Bach. The church choirs often have a high standard, and the most advanced music is performed in the churches as part of the folk church culture. Participating in church choirs is one of the biggest activities in Sweden.

Throughout the twentieth century the decision-making bodies of the church have been democratically elected and represent most walks of life. Since 1931 local parish councils have attracted the attention of the political parties, the reason being control of the tax money paid to the church. Church elections have seldom drawn great attention from the majority of the voters. Only infrequently do more than 20 percent vote, compared to 80-90 percent in general elections. The parish council decides on most matters concerning the parish. Until the year 2000, however, parish pastors were employed by the bishop and the diocesan chapter. This gave these pastors great freedom in preaching and spiritual counseling. But since 2000 pastors have been employed by the parish council, which is the only body appointing new parish pastors. The conflict of control over the pulpit has always been there. In Sweden this has historically been called the double line of responsibility: bishops and clergy had their responsibilities in the spiritual field and elected laypeople were responsible for the practical organization of church life.

Since the seventeenth century the local people have participated in elections of their parish pastors. They have also formed parish councils to decide on economic and social issues, including care of the poor people. They have always had the right to freely tax themselves to cover the expenses of the parish. The parish councils of today carry on this tradition.

The general synod of the Church of Sweden is elected every four years. Since 1982 there has been a dramatic change in its structure of 251 members. Earlier it was a continuation of the estate of the clergy, which in 1868 was replaced by a general synod, still dominated by bishops and clergy. Gradually laypeople attained more influence. The reform of 1982, as part of changed relationships to the state, was a break with historical tradition. For the first time bishops had no right to vote in the decisions of the assembly. Now the democratic principle was established as predominant, which meant, in practical terms, that the political parties dominated the scene. Nonpolitical groups were of course allowed to participate and nominate candidates. The question raised is whether there is any theological motivation for this way of decision making. Parliamentary procedures are strictly followed. The church board at the national level is appointed according to the weight of the parties in the general synod. Some people have questioned why church structure should imitate that of society at large. What is the theological reason?

In the twentieth century the death of the folk church has been predicted many times. Still it lives. It is more on the minds of people than it was around 1950. This was very evident when Archbishop K. G. Hammar (1997-), in a newspaper interview at Christmas 2002, expressed a liberal theology. Answering the question whether to become a Christian you had to believe in the virgin birth of Jesus or in the miracles of walking on water, he answered: No, that is not essential for becoming or living as a Christian. He was accused of not representing the true faith by other church leaders of a more fundamentalist standpoint. He said we need to rediscover the mysticism in Christian faith and to interpret some of the biblical stories from a poetic view. He criticized church institutions per se. To open the hearts of people to God and restore relations to humans and nature, you do not have to defend church institutions and inherited structures. The ensuing newspaper debates were the most vivid in memory, and most Swedes found themselves talking religion at coffee breaks as never before. In short, interest in religion is high in Sweden now, and the role of the folk churches has to be redefined. Structures are there, seemingly unaltered. The first chapter and this one have tried to show the historic continuity in shaping the folk church from the missionaries one thousand years ago until the present day. The church buildings and the services in them proclaim the same message now as then, though the language has changed. Its servants are as much shaped by society around them now as then.

6. *Into the Ecumenical World*

Björn Ryman

The twentieth century can be seen as the century of globalization and the century of ecumenism. Many historians have judged it the dark century, the century of holocausts, the battle against the ideologies of Nazism and communism. In the Nordic countries there is a constant reevaluation of government policy on these issues. Were our countries on the side of justice? Did we do enough? Could we have acted differently? And did the churches act differently on the ethical issues than the governments?

This chapter cannot answer all these questions, but it will deal with historical realities as they evolved. Focus is on the national churches with an emphasis on their leadership. Focus is also on the Nordic countries as an entity, although there are variations among them, particularly during the Second World War. They all had fundamentally different experiences, which really divided them. One major task for church leadership was to try and keep in contact during the war years and to heal the wounds after the war. Another focus will be the wholehearted support of the Nordic countries for international church bodies like the World Council of Churches (WCC), the Lutheran World Federation (LWF), and the Conference of European Churches (CEC).

The Prewar Years

The heritage of Nathan Söderblom was vivid in Scandinavia. Those who were present at the 1925 ecumenical meeting in Stockholm resolved themselves to a great degree to carry the work forward. One of them, Eivind Berggrav, acted as a journalist during the meeting. Later on he would become bishop of Oslo. He was superenthusiastic about the meeting in Stockholm and Uppsala. When hearing about Söderblom's death, he hurried to the funeral in Uppsala. "I felt the world became poorer and heaven richer" was his first reaction. A new era came into his life, he explained. He likened his experience at the funeral to that of the apostles at Mount Tabor, seeing the transfiguration of Jesus. He saw it as a personal summons to continue the work of Söderblom internationally.

Söderblom had been present in Vadstena in 1895 when the World Student Christian Federation was founded in an ecumenical spirit. This student movement became a planting school for the growth of the ecumenical movement, and influenced many of the leaders of the Nordic churches we will meet in this chapter. It had a twin organization in the Young Men's Christian Association, which was established in all Nordic countries at the same time. It represented a kind of alliance ecumenism with concrete programs on the grassroots level, particularly when young people moved from rural into urban areas. Another form of ecumenism was represented by the experiences of the missionaries, who on the field cooperated among themselves regardless of confession. All these experiences were translated on to the Nordic landscape at the turn of the twentieth century.

In Sweden, Erling Eidem succeeded Söderblom as archbishop in 1932. He had been a professor in Lund in southern Sweden, which is close to Germany. The new nationalistic influences were felt in Lund. Some theologians showed sympathy to the new regime and to the national church in Germany. Most of the professors, like Gustaf Aulén and Yngve Brilioth, took a clear stand from the beginning and distanced themselves from these tendencies. Brilioth said of the new *Reichsbischof* in Germany, "To call him a bishop seems a blasphemy." Instead he developed a working relationship with a group of ecumenically committed theologians who would carry on the work of Söderblom. This was of great importance to the new archbishop, Eidem, who was inexperienced in international affairs. This group tried to pilot the Church of Sweden through the storms leading up to WWII. Although formal links were kept to the Protestant churches of Germany, the main thrust was toward the ecumenical movement then being formed, and particularly to its ties to the Church of England. A heavy responsibility fell on Brilioth, who had most affinity to George Bell, bishop of Chichester and a formal leader of the ecumenical movement in formation. Sweden as a neutral country was then used as a mailbox or meeting place between the opposing nations. It must be understood that some of Archbishop Eidem's meetings with German counterparts, even with Adolf Hitler himself in 1934, were done on behalf of the whole ecumenical movement and always in accordance with Bishop Bell.

Brilioth was professor and bishop and, from 1950 on, archbishop just like his father-in-law, Nathan Söderblom. His main thrust toward the Anglican tradition was exemplified in two major works: *Eucharistic Faith and Practice* and *The Anglican Revival*. He represented Sweden at the first Faith and Order conference in Lausanne (1927). He was also present in Prague in 1928 when the three branches of the ecumenical movement met for a working conference: World Alliance, Faith and Order, and Life and Work.

One step in strengthening the ecumenical agenda in Sweden was the formation of the Swedish Ecumenical Council in 1933. One of its first public statements was to protest against the Aryan Paragraph introduced in Germany. A Scandinavian ecumenical magazine had been launched by this group, called *Kristen Gemenskap*. The council provided news of the church struggle in Germany and had good contacts to the Confessing Church and to Dietrich Bonhoeffer, who visited Sweden twice.

During the 1930s many Scandinavian bishops and professors participated actively in all the major ecumenical conferences, particularly in Edinburgh and Oxford, and a preparatory meeting in Hampstead. As the German churches decided not to participate, it fell on Archbishop Eidem to convey messages to them from these meetings. As a kind of protest, he said the intercessional prayers in German during the solemn concluding service at Saint Paul's Cathedral. It is true to say that the contributions by Scandinavian theologians to these ecumenical meetings were substantial.

The democratic nations of the North were surrounded by totalitarian ideologies. To the east was Soviet Communism, a constant threat to Finland. To the south was German National Socialism, which very few people imagined would threaten the Nordic nations. Bolshevism was considered godless, and most church people were staunch anticommunists. But before 1938 National Socialism was considered by some people, even clergy, an ideology for strengthening the nation morally, giving a sense of purpose to the nation, and rebuilding Germany, which had been near ruin. In free elections in Sweden, never more than 0.7 percent voted for the Nazi Party, in Norway maybe 1.5 percent. The numbers were never great, but later historical research has taken great pains in uncovering as many sympathizers as possible toward Germany. Officially the Nordic countries strained themselves in upholding formal relations with Germany promoting sports and music exchanges even during the war years, as Germany was the biggest trading partner and the center for culture. Unofficially most Nordic people tried to keep uncontaminated by the new influences from Germany.

The church leadership, supported by the churchgoing people, took some initiative for reconciliation and peace. The belief was that the Nordic North should be a reconciler of nations. Many big meetings and several church diplomatic missions were made in 1938-39 to try to avoid the big war coming. Foremost in this endeavor was Berggrav, at this time vice president of the World Alliance for Promoting International Friendship through the Churches. Like several of his Scandinavian counterparts, he had studied theology in Germany and knew several of the theologians there, as well as Ernst von Weizäcker, diplomat in the foreign office of Germany. The first week of September 1939 Berggrav gathered a few men in Oslo around a statement of peace. Its pious title was "God's Calling to Us Now." It was considered a great miracle in Norway that the leader of the more fundamentalist wing of the church there, Ole Hallesby, signed it together with his more liberal theological foe, Bishop Berggrav.

Björn Ryman

With Berggrav as the central actor, furious diplomatic activity developed with travels to England and Germany. It even reached the royal families of Scandinavia, who met together in Stockholm making an overture for peace. Berggrav's hectic travels and meetings with many personalities established him as the international and ecumenical spokesman for the Scandinavian churches. In a book he summarized his experiences as "In vain for peace." All efforts had been in vain.

The War Years

First, Finland was attacked by Stalin's Soviet Union in November 1939. This could happen because of the pact between Germany and the Soviet Union. Stalin could move into Finland and Hitler into Poland and the Baltic countries. The Finnish soldiers fought bravely on their skis in the Winter War, causing much damage to Stalin's big but untrained army. The Finnish government had hoped Sweden and other countries would come to their rescue, but the Swedish Social Democratic government said no to official military intervention but sanctioned voluntary military assistance. Finns were frustrated by this decision, but public opinion in Sweden has never been so strong for the cause of Finland as during the Winter War. Many young men rallied to fight on the side of the Finns, including several from the Christian student movement, like three sons of Söderblom's. Most Scandinavians expressed strong anticommunist feelings at this time. Finally Finland's army had to surrender. Important land areas were handed over to the Russians. The people of Finland were poorer than ever and had to take care of half a million refugees. In this time of national peril the Evangelical Lutheran Church was seen as something of a lifesaver for the people of Finland. God through his church was considered life insurance for the nation. The Finns survived despite all odds as an independent nation.

At this hour of greatest peril a new initiative was taken that would be a catalyst for Nordic ecumenism for decades to come. In 1940, in the thousand-year-old city of Sigtuna, close to Stockholm and Uppsala, the Nordic Ecumenical Institute (NEI) was founded. The real enthusiast for this was the leader of the lay academy at Sigtuna, Manfred Björkquist (1884-1985). As a spiritual heir to Söderblom, he was a founder and leader of numerous church enterprises, such as the Sigtuna foundation and a folk high school. These institutes were financed by private sponsors. This was also the case for the NEI. Although the folk churches of the four countries were the founders and members of the board, they had very little money for new ventures, particularly in the ecumenical sphere. Because they were state churches, all money was locked into parish work. Also participating from the beginning were the free churches, which were members of the Swedish Ecumenical Council.

The institute at Sigtuna had only two employees, Director Nils Ehrenström and his assistant, Harry Johansson. Since 1930 Ehrenström had been employed in research for the ecumenical movement in Geneva. He was sent there by Söderblom, and he was instrumental in shaping many of the documents leading up to the formal establishment of the WCC in 1948. He and Johansson were the first two professional ecumenists in Scandinavia. Money for their services had to be sought in a new way. Their mandate was enormous. They traveled together on their first mission to Copenhagen. They were going to meet the chairperson of the institute, who was the rector of the University of Copenhagen, professor of theology Jens Nørregaard. (See the biographical sketch of Nørregaard in chapter 9.) They were going to set the ecumenical agenda for the future.

The next morning in Copenhagen they woke up to the invasion of German soldiers, who on April 9, 1940, occupied Denmark and Norway. A totalitarian military state had by a surprise move with precision and in secret managed to crush two democracies. The attacks were totally unprovoked. A dictatorship based on a race ideology and blind obedience to the leader had triumphed over small, undefended nations. Our three ecumenists were sitting in the storm center of world politics. They felt their calling to the ecumenical task had been confirmed.

At this meeting they tried to develop a strategy of keeping the information moving through secret channels. The ecumenical magazine *Kristen Gemenskap* (Christian community) was one means of communication that was successfully used during the occupation years. The foremost task of the NEI was to try and keep the Nordic churches together during the war years. Modes of communication had been established already from the fateful day of occupation, April 9, 1940.

A second task for the NEI was looking after the worldwide ecumenical movement and its office in Geneva. As neutral Switzerland was surrounded by the Axis powers in 1940, and there was great fear that mail could not leave Switzerland to the Allied powers, those in Geneva decided that Sigtuna in Sweden should be an alternate, emergency location for what would become the WCC. This never occurred. The plan materialized insofar as copies of all documents were sent to Sigtuna and correspondence to certain countries was forwarded by Sigtuna. At the same time, the NEI kept in close contact with London and New York. In these countries national councils of churches had been initiated as counterparts to the WCC. In Britain George Bell, bishop of Chichester, was the visionary and driving force. In the United States John Foster Dulles was called "Mr. Layman" or "Mr. Protestant" for his deep involvement in the ecumenical movement up to its formation in 1948. In these ecumenical centers concerted study projects were conducted by very active intellectuals, theologians, and professionals, in mapping out the role of the churches for peace and reconstruction after the war. They corresponded with each other — Geneva, London, New York, and Sigtuna — exchanging drafts of their studies.

A type of think tank was established for the NEI in 1942. This study group worked for a couple years on a document called "Swedish Memorandum on Christian Guidelines on the Reconstruction Work after the War." From a perspective of social ethics, it is interesting to analyze the thoughts that sprang up during the darkest years in Europe. The first sentence reads: "It makes a difference for a Christian person how the political problems are solved." *Pax et Justitia* — peace and justice — were the ideals. "The Swedish line is a Christian line" was a slogan during the war. This document connects in its title to this slogan. The main points of the document are:

> "Our first question is: How shall the participation of the churches in the aid work best be organized?" This is treated in the chapter entitled

"Mutual Aid." A second question appears: "How shall the respect for justice and liberty be maintained and develop among the democracies in the present state under pressure?" This is treated in the chapter "Future of Democracy." The parallel question is: How shall this respect be restored in Germany? This is discussed in the chapter "Treatment of Germany and Punishment of War Criminals." The fourth question concludes: "How shall peace and justice be prevailing in the life of the states?" This will be dealt with in the chapter on the international order of justice.

On the treatment of Germany, the authors state that the value of human life had rested on unsafe pillars and that a tradition of democracy never took root prior to the new order of Nazism. From their own experiences the group writes: "In fairness one should not forget that there has really existed a resistance movement even inside Germany and that many individuals tried to fight Nazism according to their strength and that, because of this, they became martyrs for their conviction. But the opposition never turned into a popular movement." Quite forward-looking is the following sentence: "Finally we should keep in mind that no other measures are defensible than those whose final aim is that Germany can be taken up as an equal member of the European community."

These thoughts were shared with equals in the ecumenical movement in Geneva, London, and New York, where similar study projects were conducted. During the worst war years there was a strategy from the ecumenical movement to stay together and plan for reconstruction and peace.

Resistance Movements

The third task of the NEI was to try and keep in contact with people connected to the resistance in Germany. It was in Sigtuna that the famous meeting between Bishop Bell and Dietrich Bonhoeffer of the Confessing Church in Germany took place. Bell was on an official visit to the Anglican congregations in Sweden, and the meeting was suddenly and secretly arranged. However, the British war cabinet was never convinced that there existed a genuine resistance movement in Germany. Some of these Germans risked their lives meeting people from the institute at the height of the war. Four of these Christian personalities had the opportunity to travel in German service to the Scandinavian countries during the war. They were part of the Kreisau group, which met at the castle of Helmuth James von Moltke in Schlesien. They were:

- Eugen Gerstenmaier, in the foreign office of the church, imprisoned after the July 20 coup and released from prison by the Allies; he initiated Evangelisches Hilfswerk in 1945.
- Helmuth James von Moltke, in Auswärtiges Amt and leader of the Kreisau group, named after his family estate, imprisoned January 19, 1944, sentenced to death and executed January 23, 1945.
- Theodor Steltzer, served in Norway from 1940 to 1944 on Falkenhorst's staff, sentenced to death after July 20, through intervention of the Sigtuna group saved from execution and released from prison May 1945.
- Adam von Trott zu Solz, colleague of von Moltke in Auswärtiges Amt, sentenced to death and executed August 26, 1944.

For the Scandinavians Steltzer was the most important. As a transport officer in Norway he was free to travel to Sweden and made it a point to stop over in Sigtuna. He also served as a secret messenger between the detained bishop of Oslo, Berggrav, and the institute in Sigtuna. In this way the official Church of Norway had a chance to send messages to the outside world, when most of its clergy had refused to obey the Quisling regime. For instance, Berggrav's manuscript, written in detention, was smuggled to Sigtuna, where it was edited and printed. It was a book outlining his Christian view of society. He had developed a very critical stance against the strong state, which imposed itself on the citizens. The totalitarian Nazi regime was the apex of this strong state development. He had a strong belief in the Christian individual and the living communities Christians belonged to. The state should not necessarily impose new structures on these communities. You can discern similar ideas among his colleagues, the Scandinavian bishops. They were of a common mind in rejecting totalitarian regimes.

The NEI also received a fourth task: to help bind the wounds that had been inflicted. Occupied Norway felt resentment toward Finland. They looked upon Finland as a collaborator with their enemy, the Germans. Norwegians failed to appreciate the fact that Finland feared being swallowed by the Soviet Union. Amidst political turmoil, little Finland was torn between Germany and Russia. Officials from the German church had participated in a bishop consecration in Finland. Bishop Berggrav was also upset that there were Christians in Sweden who had supported the Germans during the war. Therefore he did not want to have the first official meeting after the war take place in Sweden. That had been the idea for starting a new chapter of reconstruction and reconciliation. Instead, the reconciliatory meeting took place in Copenhagen in August 1945.

The importance of religion increased during the war years. The churches tried to assist people in need in the midst of great insecurity. This entailed both spiritual and material assistance. Sweden managed to send food and clothing to Norway and Finland, and to an extent even weapons and volunteers to Finland. In occupied Denmark and Norway the church in several instances sided on human rights issues against the oppression of the occupying power. Bishop Berggrav, for example, demanded that the powers of occupation respect the Hague convention.

The war was a unifying factor for the people of Finland, as it bridged to a large degree the internal division created by the civil war in 1918. The church identified itself with the people and showed solidarity with the political and the military leadership.

Postwar Reconstruction

Many pertinent issues were discussed at the 1945 meeting in Copenhagen, but all problems were not solved between the churches. There were more complications regarding Finland's difficult situation. Time had to mend that wound. The indignation of the Norwegians against Sweden's breach of neutrality in letting German troops pass in transit was still vigorous. Sweden managed to stay out of the war thanks to that breach of neutrality. The government felt pressed to give in to German demands in letting troops through and in exporting iron ore. Some considered this a wise policy, others saw it as a defeat and betrayal of democratic values. These outstanding issues causing bitterness between neighbors had to be dealt with in an honest way. More meetings in a conciliatory mood had to take place.

To build up what had been destroyed was a genuine wish by all. Most hard hit by war was of course Finland. Many of its children had spent a couple years in Sweden or Denmark during the war. Most of them returned, but some remained with their new families. The eastern part of Finland was lost to Russia in the peace agreement of 1944. This also meant that 420,000 refugees had to be resettled. Most of them were allotted small pieces of land for agriculture. Apart from the human and economic losses in the war, all Finns had to contribute both to the war reparations paid to the Soviet Union and to the most needy of their own population. Here the Lutheran church played a role through its parishes all across the country. In every parish there was a deacon or deaconess for the parishioners' social and spiritual needs. The church acted as a servant of the people. Particular attention was given to the war invalids and war widows. In this way the *diaconia* of the church grew strong, which meant that education of the deacons was stressed.

Finland also received assistance from abroad, which was channeled through the parishes. The American Lutherans along with the Quakers were large contributors to this effort. The leading American Lutherans were the same as those who forcefully endorsed a new start for the LWF. They visited Finland in 1946 after a meeting of church leaders in Uppsala. Some of this aid was used in a strategic way to build centers for education of church workers. Ideologically, the contacts with the American churches were important. Theologically, most contacts had been with the German theologians, which was also the case during the war. The new archbishop, Aleksi Lehtonen, was pro-Anglican but realized that the economic assistance offered by American Lutherans was important. Through the currency exchange regulations, it was possible to triple the value of the aid by importing sugar and coffee.

The reconstruction of Finland was accomplished through national self-reliance, with the international church aid being an inspiring complement. The Finnish Lutheran Church was strengthened as a national church by the way it organized its relief work after the war. The character of a church for all its people was stressed theologically and through revivals. These thoughts were heralded by the young clergymen, who had served as chaplains at the war front.

Norway had also suffered through the war years. Norwegian resistance to the German occupation was extraordinarily strong. The first WWII defeat anywhere for the German forces occurred in May 1940 in Narvik. Malnourishment took its toll on the population during the tough occupation, particularly in Oslo. The only food supply possible from outside the country was food aid shipped by train from Sweden. As the Swedes did not wish it to come into German hands, it was shipped to the Swedish congregation in Oslo, whose two pastors were responsible for its distribution. After a few months the small diaspora congregation was handling enormous quantities of food, but it was the only food aid available in very meager circumstances. The Swedish vicar, Axel Weebe, wrote a diary during the war years, describing the situation in detail, including negotiations with both the Quisling regime and the German occupiers. He was able to visit the prisoners, including Bishop Berggrav. Fifty years later his notes were made available as a book.

Most devastated was the northernmost part of Norway, Finnmark, where the German forces burned churches, twenty-six out of forty-six, and parish buildings as they were withdrawing from Finland during the last months of the war. Appeals for aid went out to the ecumenical partners. There was a response to this, although Norway used its own resources to restore the church and the country to the prewar level. This happened astonishingly quickly within a two-year period. The diaconal institutions in the parishes played a key role, like they did in Finland. Unlike Finland, though, the national church of Norway was not strengthened as a church for the people after the war. In Finland the state needed the church to rebuild the nation, while in Norway the postwar state under Social Democratic leadership wished to have only secular institutions in society, where the church influence on society was minimal.

Denmark and Sweden incurred no war damage to speak of. Instead, the war-torn countries turned to them for aid. Since 1922 Denmark had a well-organized institution called Emergency Aid to the Evangelical Churches in Europe. For thirty years its leadership was tied to its founder, a church social activist, Doctor of Theology Alfred Th. Jørgensen. In the 1920s its main activities were coordinated with the American Protestant Federal Council. Through fund-raising activities within the national church in Denmark, it emerged as the giving arm of the folk church. Its recipients were primarily Lutheran congregations in central Europe. After the depression in 1929, it took a leading role in Protestant relief efforts. Jørgensen was also an active member of the Lutheran World Convention. Danish Emergency Aid managed to steer a politically correct course, as Nazi Germany expanded ideologically and militarily in the areas of Protestant minority churches in central Europe. During the war humanitarian aid was directed to Finland, particularly its children. After the war the rampant devastation of many European countries called for an expansion of the operation.

In Sweden there was only the major Lutheran church, which was not affected by the war. Many eyes turned to neutral Sweden for aid and inspiration. For this reason Archbishop Eidem called church leaders from the major Lutheran churches to a meeting. It took place July 24-26, 1946, at the deaconess institution, Samariterhemmet in Uppsala. The official representative of the Lutheran churches in Germany greeted for the first time since the war on foreign soil the leaders of the Scandinavian and American churches. Bishop Hans Meiser of Munich represented a country that had waged war against all the Nordic countries except Sweden. He had traveled for several days and was too late for the beginning of the meeting, but it was prolonged. Eidem welcomed him in German:

> There are meetings in life, dear brother, when we must meet with sad hearts. A heavy burden has fallen upon us and upon all mankind. We want to do what Saint Paul said in the lesson we have just read: "Bear

ye one another's burden." We know that your country is bearing heavy burdens. All of us must bear our share of the responsibility. We do not wish to judge. "Love rules our hearts." I want you to be firmly convinced of this that we receive you in our midst with brotherly love.

Bishop Meiser gave a long and humble response to this greeting:

You must believe me that I have come here with a deep feeling of gratitude and am now deeply moved that I can be here and hear these words of welcome. You cannot imagine how I have missed the broken relation in the past years. We know of so much injustice that has been done by our people and we could not prevent it. We fully realize that the collapse of the Hitler regime was possible only through the terrible destruction which had to come. We have documentary evidence now, that should Hitler have been victorious the real difficulties of the Church would have just begun. We trembled at what would follow, if Hitler would have won. With the collapse there came a real religious experience. It was evident amongst our people. Never were the churches so crowded before. Now we must place ourselves before the judgement of God. We dare not confess the faults of others, but only our own. We accept all this as the judgment of God because our nation treated the Jews as we did. As our own churches burned and were destroyed we remembered that the German people first set fire to the Jewish synagogues. . . . Certainly we knew of some of the terrible conditions which prevailed in our own concentration camps, some knew much more than others. Now we must come to a full realization of how we can repent and ask God to forgive.

This declaration of guilt was of decisive importance for future work. The representatives of the German churches publicly denounced everything that had any connection to National Socialism. Meiser also confessed the guilt of the German church in the treatment of the Jews under Nazi rule. Archbishop Eidem was the leader who welcomed the Germans back into the Christian community. This played a part in the reconciliation that was necessary between former enemy countries.

Nordic church leaders who met in Geneva in 1946 to plan reconstruction included Erling Eidem, Archbishop of Sweden; Eivind Berggrav, primate of Norway; and Yngve Brilioth, who was to become Archbishop of Sweden in 1950.

Lutheran World Federation

This meeting in 1946 was of decisive importance for the formation of the Lutheran World Federation (LWF). The guidelines for this body were drawn up at this meeting. The American Lutherans had immediately after the war started large-scale aid projects to strengthen the war-damaged churches. This was true for the minority churches in Eastern Europe as well as for the Western occupation zones of Germany. Although emergency aid often dominated organizational matters on the agenda, the American Lutherans were genuinely interested in revitalizing Lutheran theology. Most people felt that traditional German Lutheran theology had suffered a serious blow during the Third Reich, particularly in how the doctrine of the two kingdoms was misused. As a consequence there were great expectations on Nordic theologians for a renewal of Lutheran theology. Here the Lundensian theology of Anders Nygren (see the portrait in chapter 9) and the theological presuppositions against the strong state, expressed by Berggrav during and after the war, were favored by the Americans. Nygren became the first president of the LWF, and served in its department of theology until 1957. At the meeting in Uppsala it was decided to hold a general assembly in Lund in 1947. Two of the main speakers at this first big international church assembly after the war were Nygren and Berggrav. Nygren gave a keynote address for the whole assembly. He finished with the slogan: "Forward to Luther!" This became a guideline for the new church cooperation in the LWF. Berggrav spoke in a church service one evening.

"If anyone is persecuted and tortured because of his convictions and without any legal grounds, the church, as the guardian of the human conscience, must stand solidly on the side of the sufferers," said Berggrav in his speech entitled "Christ and the World Drama." "A truly evangelical church must take a stand against any attempt to interfere with or subjugate the individual conscience by the exercise of authority or violence," continued the Norwegian bishop under the dome of Lund. He spoke from his own experience: "And if individual units or persons be displaced against their will and be made to suffer because of a firmly based conviction common to many believers, the Church must not and cannot act as if it did not concern her. The body of Christ would suffer." Berggrav founded this appeal to clearly protest injustices and oppression on his own experience and that of the Norwegian church during the war, but also on biblical and Lutheran tradition. Together with the German bishop Hanns Lilje, who had also been imprisoned during the war, they gave witness one evening in Lund. "It was a moment which, with the strength of revelation, the foundation for the deep influence of the two men's spiritual power became known," wrote one observer in the newspaper.

All the Nordic churches participated in the formation of the LWF. Denmark and Sweden played a more active role than Norway and Finland, which were most affected by the war. Iceland also became a member. The folk churches from the five Nordic countries should in the future serve faithfully in the federation. Their combined support of it has been substantial, and during some years they have been the greatest economic contributors. Theologians from all countries have made major contributions, particularly regarding Martin Luther research like Regin Prenter of Aarhus. Only one person from the Nordic countries has served as general secretary, and that is Gunnar Stålsett, theologian from Kirkenes in the far north. He served from 1985 to 1994, when the issues of peace and justice were high on the agenda.

World Council of Churches

The major ecumenical postwar event was the formation of the World Council of Churches (WCC) in Amsterdam in 1948. As we have seen, the NEI was extremely active in its formation phase, interrupted by the war. A custom developed whereby the Nordic member churches coordinated their preparatory work before each assembly or commission meeting through the NEI. The Nordic folk churches were not formally one bloc in the WCC, but in reality they performed as one unit, interchanging positions between them. For instance, Eidem was elected president in 1948. When he resigned in 1950, Berggrav replaced him. Throughout the century there have been one Scandinavian at the top and other representatives in the central committee and other bodies on a rotational basis.

The Nordic folk churches also liaised with other Lutheran churches. In the beginning there was the idea that the different confessional families should be the main structure for the membership of the WCC. The American Lutherans tried to enact this idea before the Amsterdam assembly. It was not accepted as a principle, although most elections to different ecumenical bodies followed confessional lines. Anglicans, Reformed, Lutherans, Congregationalists — all were allotted seats and influence in different committees according to strength.

Another conference of great significance was the meeting of the Faith and Order Commission in Lund in 1952. Archbishop Brilioth presided together with Bishop Nygren of Lund and Gustaf Aulén, Strängnäs. They had served together on the theological faculty in the 1930s. One participant commented on Brilioth's presidency: "He presided in the scene of his own early triumphs as a theologian, a prophet with honor in his own country." On behalf of the WCC, he had visited the Orthodox and the Oriental churches in the Middle East in 1947, inviting them to the first general assembly of the WCC. They accepted the invitation and became members. Brilioth's greatest ecumenical partner had been George Bell of the Anglican Communion. Much of his theological writing centered on ecclesiological questions such as the roles of a bishop and the significance of Eucharist in the Anglican and Lutheran traditions. This conference in 1952 was a crowning experience for him. Although Nygren saw to it that there was a common Lutheran witness and input into the ecumenical agenda in the 1950s, a general shift can be noticed. From then on the Anglican tradition with a stress on apostolic succession, the role of a bishop, and the liturgy put a significant mark on ecumenical conversations, first and foremost in Sweden, then in Finland, Norway, and Iceland, and only to some extent in Denmark. Due to the experiences of the Reformation, Sweden and Finland had a more advantageous position, closer to the Anglican tradition. The western part of Scandinavia had strangely enough a longer road to travel theologically in rapprochement to the Anglican tradition. The Faith and Order conference in 1952 set two study projects in motion, on ecclesiology and on baptism. The latter produced the document *One Lord — One Baptism*. The motto of this conference was "Not to do separately what can be done together."

United Nations General Secretary Dag Hammarskjöld (center) at Evanston, Illinois, where he addressed the World Council of Churches general assembly in
1954. On the right is Archbishop Geoffrey Fisher of Canterbury and on the left
is Dr. Frederick Nolde, secretary of the Churches Commission on International
Affairs, who was involved in shaping the UN Declaration of Human Rights in
1948. Hammarskjöld´s friend from his student days in Uppsala, Yngve Brilioth,
Archbishop of Sweden from 1950 to 1958, invited him to the general assembly.
Photo: WCC.

The next WCC general assembly was held in the United States, in Evanston, Illinois, in 1954, and can be judged as the epitome of American influence in organized ecumenism. The American Protestant churches had been leading in organizational and financial matters and had built a huge center on Manhattan for the National Council of Churches in Christ. The Scandinavian folk churches, with their ties to and regulations from the state, did not possess the skills and abilities of the American churches to organize and raise funds. This was something they had to learn. Many of those Scandinavians in the forefront of the assemblies had other qualifications. Foremost of these were probably their theological qualifications, their heritage as folk churches, and their authority as leaders. The Nordic countries also had the advantage of being between the two ideological blocs and having stood outside the colonial race. This was true of the two first general secretaries of the United Nations, Tryggve Lie of Norway, who resigned in 1952, and Dag Hammarskjöld, who was appointed to the world's toughest job in April 1953. He was a main speaker at the Evanston Assembly. No one knew at that time that he was a religious man, thinking deeply about the existential questions, drawing himself to mysticism. He was engaged as speaker to the assembly by his friend from student days in Uppsala, Yngve Brilioth. They had both served at the 1925 ecumenical meeting in Sweden. Since his tragic death in Zambia in 1961, Hammarskjöld has become known mostly for his reflections, published posthumously under the title *Markings*. To a bewildered cultural elite, distanced from Christianity and mysticism, the theological and mystical meaning of *Markings* was explained by Gustaf Aulén, followed by many others. In one sense Hammarskjöld was a genuine product of the folk church concept through his upbringing. This religious base took him to the mystics and the reflections of his own destiny.

Nordic-German Church Convent

Another ecumenical endeavor was a Norwegian initiative in 1949. Norwegian laymen — Conrad Bonnevie-Svendsen and Henrik Hauge, active both in the resistance movement during the war and in church reconstruction work afterward — made an astonishing move. They suggested that the Church of Norway cooperate formally with the German evangelical churches. To invite the former enemy and occupation power into such a venture seemed at that time very far-fetched. People of the church saw it as a sign of reconciliation. There was a vision of a community building confidence, leading to peace between enemy nations. The initiative was called the Nordic-German Church Convent. All five folk churches of the Nordic countries participated along with the common undivided Evangelical Church in Germany. The first meeting, or convent, took place in Copenhagen, November 3-4, 1949. In Copenhagen an activist clergyman, Halfdan Høgsbro, found himself in the center of activities from the beginning. He became bishop in 1950, and as such attended most of the convents. He had, on a voluntary basis, been responsible for refugee camps for Germans on the Danish-German border in Schleswig at the end of the war. He also cofounded the Ecumenical Council of Denmark, which included Catholics and Mennonites. They in turn formed a committee called Church Service for Refugees in Denmark, which was changed in 1956 to the Danish Refugee Council. As Christians they felt compelled to serve the interned German refugees, however guilty they might feel. It is the command of Christ that his gospel be preached to all human beings, including those of his creation who were now internees. In the one thousand camps many Danish clergymen served along with German evangelical pastors as well as thirty Catholic priests. Among other initiatives, Høgsbro helped to organize refugee service inside Germany and also a big national fund drive through collection in churches for German refugees. In the beginning such initiatives were regarded as treason by some. In the end they heralded a new era of reconciliation among former war enemies. The Nordic folk churches tried to follow the path of reconciliation, paved by church leaders before the war. In this spirit of reconciliation and community building, the Nordic-German Church Convent got on its way. The initiators had worked with German representatives of the resistance movement during the war. Now they worked for a new Germany rising out of the ashes of the old.

The Nordic-German Church Convent continued to meet regularly in the Nordic countries and in Germany. Often there were theological deliberations on the agenda. The participants made it a point also to meet in the German Democratic Republic (GDR). These meetings had great significance, for they made it possible for the church in the GDR to get space to maneuver in a hostile environment. It is also true that the churches could be exploited by the GDR government to further its political aims. But the organization took the risk, and convened about seventy times before the Berlin Wall fell. They prepared for these meetings openly and went through all the official bureaucracy concerning travel permits, etc. The churches in the GDR felt a stimulus to get some open space to conduct their regular church work in a better environment.

Conference of European Churches

Another ecumenical initiative along the same lines with strong links to the folk church of Denmark was the formation of the Conference of European Churches (CEC). Again Halfdan Høgsbro welcomed guests to Denmark, this time eight years after the Nordic-German meeting. The purpose this time was to found an organization that would make it possible for the churches with a common European history to meet despite being separated by the Iron Curtain. The first official CEC meeting was held in Denmark in 1959. In the beginning the conference was important to the churches living under real socialism in Eastern Europe as well as Protestant minority churches in southern Europe. The first three conferences were held in Denmark. The CEC got a new mandate when the Iron Curtain fell in 1989, and when most European countries decided to join the European Union. The group's beginning was a risky initiative, and members even had to meet on a boat in international waters in the Baltic Sea, as entrance and exit visas were not easily obtained. From its humble beginnings, the CEC continued to grow in influence and held a major assembly in Trondheim in 2003.

The Nordic-German Church Convent and the CEC are examples of organizations that tried to cross the Iron Curtain openly and officially. One of their aims was to make it possible for church representatives in the East to travel abroad and make new contacts. The Nordic folk churches supported this line of action. This was also the case with the WCC, especially after the Russian Orthodox Church joined in 1961. Already at that time this coexistence was criticized by many Christians who carried strong anticommunist sentiments and who favored those Christians who belonged to persecuted underground churches. Although most of the leaders of the folk churches at heart were anticommunist, or at least felt no affinity to the Moscow type of socialism that was forced on people, they realistically tried to exercise a church diplomacy that made it easier for churches to exist. Some have been criticized for this policy, especially by those who smuggled Bibles behind the Iron Curtain. There existed several mission organizations who specialized in such activities and developed a network of secret contacts. In most Nordic countries a more radical type of activity developed in the traces of Romanian pastor Richard Wurmbrand. Many Christians supported organizations created in his spirit. They were anticommunist in nature and they raised funds in the Nordic countries for propaganda purposes. They were not supported by the folk churches and made little progress in the Scandinavian countries. The officially registered Lutheran churches in the socialist countries were the ones getting support from the Nordic folk churches.

Church Aid Organizations

The Danish and Swedish church aid organizations did what they could with fairly limited resources to assist war-damaged churches in central Europe. This aid was channeled via the LWF and WCC in formation. The Lutherans were keen to assist their sister churches. In fact, the tracks to these churches were laid out before the war, and these churches were the easiest to get access to in the ravages after the war. The churches in Hungary and Poland, for instance, received special attention. Before the Iron Curtain closed it down, interchurch aid was possible. In Hungary there were special relations to Bishop Lajos Ordass of the Lutheran church. He had studied in Lund and knew the Scandinavian languages. He even translated religious books from Swedish and Icelandic into Hungarian.

He was influential in the LWF, and many followed his story when the authorities imprisoned him in 1948. The church leaders of the North knew him personally. This was important in his release from prison in 1956, a couple months before the revolution against the Communist oppression in Budapest.

In central Europe emergency aid and pastoral care was a priority. Fifteen million Lutherans were refugees or displaced persons, the latter term being given to those who had no homeland to which to return. Some of them came to Scandinavia and stayed there. Around 25,000 Estonians and Latvians fled to Sweden in 1944-45. The Estonian church in exile organized its headquarters in Stockholm. The church and its bishop received support from the Church of Sweden. In the 1970s the Church of Sweden also had official contacts with the Estonian Evangelical Lutheran Church in Tallinn. This caused a conflict with the Estonians in Sweden. In the 1990s the Iron Curtain was gone and Estonia became once more a free and independent country, and church relations returned to normal.

In Poland, just a few hours by sea from southern Sweden, there were special links before the war with the minority church of Lutheran confession. The Swedish Seaman's church in Gdynia was important, and it continued its work right through the war and the ensuing Communist regimes, in fact being the only Seaman's church in a Communist country. Its pastor before the war, Daniel Cederberg, kept the links to the Lutherans during the war and established aid shipments to the Lutherans in the lake district of Masuria. Even the American Lutherans shipped loads of aid to this district. The devastation in Poland was total. The number of Lutherans there decreased, as many fled westward. Since the days of the Counter-Reformation Lutherans had felt an inferiority complex to the large Roman Catholic Church. As the general sentiment was that a real nationalistic Pole should also be a Catholic, Lutherans turned anti-Catholic. They longed for ties to the large Lutheran folk churches of Scandinavia. To some extent they received this, including the reconstruction of the large dome in Warsaw.

This aid to Poland became the first endeavor of the aid organization Lutherhjälpen. The name was given during the LWF assembly in Lund during the summer of 1947, and the group was strongly linked to the LWF. A common effort of the LWF in the beginning was refugee aid. Both the border changes caused by World War II and the new, sharp ideological borders created by the Iron and Bamboo curtains as well as the borders of the new state of Israel in the midst of an Arab population created streams of refugees which the world had never before experienced. In all these areas the LWF and the Nordic church aid organizations became involved.

The Nordic church aid to Germany was mainly done through the newly established Evangelisches Hilfswerk. Eugen Gerstenmaier is credited as its founder. He had visited the NEI during the war and was part of the Kreisau group and the July 20 coup against Hitler. Because of his close contacts with Scandinavia and the churches, there was an enormous influx of aid from the Scandinavian churches to the reconstruction of Germany from 1945 up to 1952. This aid was crucial in the beginning, as the Allied powers did not allow shipments to Germany. Many Germans starved to death the first year after the war. Through his good contacts with the churches in Sweden, Gerstenmaier managed to organize a large aid enterprise. Church leaders in Scandinavia considered Gerstenmaier and Evangelisches Hilfswerk to be part of the resistance to Hitler. The Left heavily criticized church aid to defeated Germany. The churches saw it as an ecumenical endeavor toward reconciliation and reconstruction for a new Europe. The high point of these close ties between German and Scandinavian churches came in Hanover in 1952, when the LWF held its second assembly, attended by 50,000 Germans. This was after the reconstruction period and shortly before the so-called economic miracle of West Germany began. It is appropriate to consider the mid-1950s as the cutting of the close German-Nordic ties that had existed since the Reformation. In one sense Hitler and World War II destroyed these special and natural relations. In another sense the afterwar experience deepened the ties between the churches, as we have seen above. When the reconciliation and reconstruction period concluded around 1955, the Nordic churches turned their eyes and ears elsewhere.

It is an irony of history that when the European Economic Community originated in Rome in 1957, the Nordic countries and churches more or less left their European involvement. In one sense particularly, the left wing in Scandinavia felt the original six member countries were tainted by the abhorrent Cs: colonialists, Catholics, capitalists, and anticommunists. This did not fit into the Scandinavian welfare model and its reformist tradition against reactionary forces. The Scandinavian countries had developed their sovereign nation-states according to a reformist social democracy. The welfare state and state intervention from the cradle to the grave was the motto, first of all in Sweden, then in the other Nordic countries. The strong society was a theme in Swedish society, which was abandoned around 1990.

Instead, the Nordic churches started to discover the churches in the Southern Hemisphere. In one sense it is true that the missionary organizations had vivid connections to their respective mission fields. These were gradually transformed to independent and indigenous churches. To some the change came abruptly in the 1960s, when the wind of change swept through Africa. A new dawn broke in 1961 in New Delhi, when both the International Missionary Council and the Russian Orthodox Church joined the WCC. For the agenda of ecumenical bodies this meant that the attention of the churches in the North turned much more to the Third World, as this part of the world now became known. The acceptance of the Russian Orthodox Church meant also a shift in church diplomacy. The Nordic churches were basically anticommunist during the early Cold War years, and official links to churches behind the Iron Curtain were virtually nonexistent. Both these facts — churches in the South and in the East — made the geopolitical map of ecumenism different from the 1960s.

From Aid to Development

As we have seen above, all five Nordic folk churches developed church aid organizations after the war. Denmark renamed its organization Folkekirkens Nødhjælp, Danchurchaid. Norway used the same name, Kirkens Nødhjelp, Norchurchaid. Sweden continued to use the name Lutherhjälpen, later on called Church of Sweden Aid. Finland created Finnchurchaid in the 1960s, Kirkon Ulkomaanapu. Icelandic Church Aid was started in 1967 as Hjalparstofun Kirkonjar. These groups now turned from emergency aid to war-torn countries in Europe to refugees outside Europe. In the 1960s they would all be heavily involved in African countries.

Danchurchaid became heavily involved with Palestinian refugees via personnel in Jerusalem and economic assistance to the Augusta Victoria Hospital on the Mount of Olives. The United Nations Relief and Works Agency asked the LWF in 1950 to take over the running of this hospital for Palestinian refugees. This would continue for half a century. Much of the financial backing has come through the Nordic aid organizations. In the beginning, Chris Christiansen was a tireless organizer for relief work among the refugees after the first Arab-Israeli war. He also visited Sweden in 1953 to make people aware of the plight of the Palestinian refugees. These church organizations were among the first to make people conscious of the Palestinian refugee problem, which was to entangle all international bodies for half a century. Humanitarian assistance was rendered to those in need, and Scandinavians were made politically aware of a new sort of refugee. All the church aid organizations stuck to their commitment to the Palestinians through all the coming wars and diplomacy. Schools have been built and many young Palestinians have received scholarships. The Nordic folk churches wanted to contribute to peace and reconciliation in the Holy Land.

If the Middle East was the first area of aid outside Europe, Hong Kong was the second. Contrary to the image of Hong Kong in 1997, when the British "returned Hong Kong" to China, where it belonged, in 1950 the city was poor and overpopulated by refugees from China, living in shantytowns. Many missionaries were forced to leave China in 1949, but some of them continued to work in Hong Kong. The refugee service was especially geared to the street children, who were numerous. With the aid they could go to school and their parents could gradually move into apartments. This was facilitated via a sponsorship program. In the 1970s it was phased out. The examples of Hong Kong and Germany show how fast economic development can make social aid projects superfluous. This has happened in many places, but alas not in Africa, whose future seemed so bright around 1960.

When Dag Hammarskjöld died in a plane accident during mediation efforts in the Congo crisis of 1961, this tragedy touched the hearts of all Swedes and many others beyond. For Lutherhjälpen his death meant a dedication to continue his task. A woman on the staff, Birgit Bram Ohlsson, wrote an appeal that was listened to in many schools at the time: "Earlier than anybody else Hammarskjöld realized the importance of the new and poor nations for world peace and development. He gave his life in the self-sacrificing service in order to realize human rights for these people. His aim was that all the peoples of the world should make a common effort to fight the poverty and plight of this world." In memory of Hammarskjöld, an appeal started which became the biggest single campaign in Lutherhjälpen's history. Eight million Swedish crowns were raised for constructing a hospital at Moshi in northern Tanzania. When it was inaugurated by President Julius Nyerere in 1970 in the foothills of Mount Kilimanjaro, it received the official name of the Kilimanjaro Christian Medical Center.

Another example is the Joint Nordic Airlift to Biafra in 1968 under the name Nordchurchaid. In a big way the Nordic church agencies cooperated in what was then one of the largest airlifts to an emergency area suffering starvation. The Igbos in southeastern Nigeria felt discriminated against in federal Nigeria when the Muslim north killed 30,000 Igbos and forced 2 million to flee back to Biafra. Federal Nigeria was backed by Great Britain and received weapons from the Soviet Union. Biafra found little diplomatic support for its break away from Nigeria. Only Julius Nyerere and Kenneth Kaunda recognized Biafra. The Norwegian and Danish church agencies tried at an early stage to support the Igbos, and many efforts were made. During the WCC general assembly in Uppsala in July 1968, one of Biafra's foremost spokesmen was the former governor Francis Ibiam, now vice president of the WCC. All church diplomacy failed and the great powers in the UN prevented airlifts. The activists in the Nordic church agencies never rested and tried all ways, both legal and illegal, to fly in aid. One night in August 1968 a Swedish pilot, Captain Carl Gustaf von Rosen, flew a DC-7 just above sea level from the Portuguese island of São Tomé to a simple road strip in Uli, Biafra. The massive airlift started with night flights. Within twenty-four hours Nordchurchaid was established, which would develop into a huge logistical operation. Over the next fifteen months 5,300 flights would follow, carrying 63,000 tons of emergency food. Catholic and Protestant aid agencies cooperated on a grand scale. Through television starving Biafran children became a visible icon for emergency aid. The internal fighting was a war of attrition that did not end until the losers were at the brink of annihilation. Other wars were to follow in Africa with the same scenario, for which the aid agencies delivered food through expensive airlifts. Von Rosen developed the practice of air-dropping food from light aircraft in Ethiopia during the famine in 1974. The Biafran emergency put the Nordic church agencies on the front pages, and their appeals for funds found generous donors among the grass roots. They were seen as trustworthy, efficient, and nonbureaucratic.

Around 1960 development aid was in the forefront of the political agenda. The world seemed to belong to the newly independent nations that formed a strong bloc in the UN. The five Nordic countries were among the first to set up government agencies for this type of development work. In this endeavor they liaised with church organizations. Partly the reason was to get political support to set aside tax money for development aid. In a short time the goal was set at 1 percent of GNP. In the sixties this was a bold vision, but in the seventies it became reality. Sweden, Denmark, and Norway were among the first nations to reach this goal. A little later Finland reached 0.7 percent. A broad-based coalition carried this political agenda and the churches were in the forefront. When countries in Africa were chosen as partners for development, most of the nations with heavy missionary involvement from the Nordic churches were picked. Tanzania and Ethiopia are prime examples.

The parliamentary majority in the 1960s and 1970s was Social Democratic, and their ideals of equality and economic cooperation were favored. The Arusha declaration with its African socialism went in this direction. Churches in the North and the South considered the one-party state with an enlightened philosopher like Julius Nyerere at the top an ideal. Churches played an important role in poverty alleviation and educational activities in the African countries, but it was thought the state should take over the hospitals and schools just like in the Scandinavian welfare model. The poor states overextended themselves and got trapped in the debt crisis, beginning in 1980. Heavy criticism against the structural adjustment programs of the International Monetary Fund and the World Bank, from both the South and the North, not least from church representatives, did not prevent the governments and people from suffering immensely. A new development agenda was dawning in which the private entrepreneur was the main agent rather than government bureaucrats.

Many Scandinavian politicians were in the forefront within the UN system to assist developing nations. Olof Palme of Sweden has already been mentioned. His counterpart in Norway, Gro Harlem Brundtland, was one of the signatories to a UN report on development and environment, *Our Common Future*. She also served as director of the World Health Organization. (See the biographical sketches of Palme and Brundtland in chapter 9.) The Danish Liberal politician Poul Hartling ended his career as UN High Commissioner for Refugees. Already in the 1940s he was aiding refugees through Danchurchaid. The Finnish president Martti Ahtisaari served in the 1980s as the UN administrator general for Namibia. These are but a few internationally recognized Scandinavian politicians serving the UN cause for the developing world.

Around 1960 the church aid organizations turned their energies to Africa and Asia. Sometimes they cooperated with the mission organizations, sometimes they competed for funds. The population at large was conscientized about the Third World. Mission and aid organizations made common cause to alleviate poverty. In this endeavor they were favored by the governments, who set aside funds for church-supported projects. The five Nordic church aid agencies took advantage of this, mostly in Denmark and Norway, where Danchurchaid and Norwegian church aid received up to 70 percent of their income from the government. For all church agencies, however, voluntary giving via church collections and Lenten campaigns saw a tremendous increase during the 1960s. As state churches, most of their normal economic activities were dependent on tax revenues. Development assistance, however, was dependent on voluntary donations. In most parishes formal representatives were appointed to raise money for the development organizations.

The worldwide church came into ordinary parish life. The international *diaconia* was established in all Nordic churches. The church agencies had sprung from missionary, diaconal, and ecumenical roots, and they were a mixture of the three.

Since 1968, in all Nordic countries, networks have been formed to advocate for the Third World. The message was that the North needs to change its trade patterns and economic systems to further equality with the nations of the South. Heated debates and campaigns on these matters took place in most parishes. The theme was that justice cannot wait. The consumption patterns of the North should change in favor of fair trade, and economic transactions should be to the advantage of the poor nations. Foreign debts should be canceled. This agenda was applied to governments and the UN system and had great backing from the grass roots. Another such campaign was geared to the antiapartheid struggle in South Africa.

The largest involvement of the Nordic countries for regions outside themselves was for the liberation struggle in southern Africa. Politically and financially the Nordic countries supported many liberation movements in most countries in southern Africa, the so-called frontline states. Assurances were given that no church money could be used for the purchase of weapons, an accusation often heard in those days. The churches were in a unique position to support local churches inside South Africa and Namibia during the worst years of apartheid dominance. Desmond Tutu, who became the Anglican archbishop of South Africa in 1985, developed special relations to the Nordic churches from 1979 onward. Then he held his first press conference in Copenhagen, supporting sanctions in trade and investment against the South African government. As secretary-general of the South African Council of Churches, he worked out many programs of Nordic support for victims of the apartheid struggle. Tutu received an honorary doctorate of theology from the University of Uppsala and, as a Nobel laureate for peace in Oslo in 1984, his voice of Christian commitment and compassion was heard more than anyone else's. Also Nelson Mandela, in appreciation for the support he had received from the Nordic countries, from governments, churches, and people's movements, went to Sweden to thank the

Archbishop Desmond Tutu of South Africa often visited the Nordic churches to involve them in the struggle for freedom.   Photo: Jim Elfström.

people of the North on his first trip abroad after twenty-six years in captivity on Robben Island. He did so in the Cathedral of Uppsala in 1990 in a sanctuary in which many could not get a seat.

Another lasting influence has been the quest for peace. As already mentioned, the détente of the 1970s brought a general trend of nonaggression. The American defeat in Vietnam brought to an end the street demonstrations, which had flourished for several years. A new era of the Cold War started around New Year 1980 when the Soviet Union invaded Afghanistan and continued later that year when Ronald Reagan was elected president of the United States on an agenda of confrontation with the Soviet Union and a heavy rearmament of nuclear weapons. The arms race in the beginning of the 1980s reached proportions never before experienced. Both the nuclear arms proliferation and the increase of conventional arms in Europe made the world an unsafe place. In this scenario the archbishops or primates of all five Nordic folk churches invited church leaders from all Christian families, East and West, North and South, to a conference of life and peace. They had hoped the pope and Orthodox patriarchs would participate, but were satisfied that they sent very high-level delegations of active participants. The conference took place in Uppsala in April 1983. In congruence with Nathan Söderblom's conference in 1925, whose follow-up was named Life and Work, this new conference was named Life and Peace. "Confidence building" was the key phrase. The Nordic bishops had lived through the Second World War as students of theology. They were not pacifists at heart but realistic about human nature and the interests of the big powers. They were of course influenced by the peace movements in recent years and were familiar with the theory of just war. This was part of the preparation.

The Life and Peace conference was attended by 150 delegates and 230 journalists from all over the world. It was a media event and it encouraged all those working for peace at that time. The nuclear issue was at the forefront. Still, there was much attention paid to justice issues, pertinent to the delegates from the South. The document condemning the nuclear arms race was one of the strongest ever signed by so many people from all sides during the Cold War. It was not just political in content. The theology of peace was expressed both in the document and what was said during the conference. Half the time was spent in services in the cathedral and in Bible studies. The inaugural sermon was given by Cardinal Arns of São Paolo. A summary of this theology is that the Christian vision for peace does not only take into account peace between God and the human being but also peace between persons. The issue of peace includes all of humanity. This meant meddling in the politics of peace. This peace does not only mean absence of military conflicts but also the presence of justice. There can be no peace without justice. Institutionalized violence in unjust systems enslaves the world. The ethical code is not only meant for Christians. All men of good will who do not share the Christian faith can be united with Christians in creating conditions for peace.

Archbishop Olof Sundby of Uppsala was initiator of the conference. It was a private triumph for him that this gathering had taken place at that time. For all the Nordic folk churches, it made them relevant to society. Prime Minister Palme opened the conference with a speech, which he concluded by quoting the pope: the new name of peace is development. This was at a time when Sweden's relations with the Soviet Union were strained because of submarine incidents. Observers of this conference as well as participants did not judge it as having a one-sided agenda. It viewed the use of nuclear arms as a definite step toward holocaust. After that there would be no life. The conference was praised for its outspokenness. The peace programs were at the heart of all Nordic churches and societies. Although the Cold War divided them in their defense systems and alliances — the three western countries to the NATO bloc and the two eastern countries being neutral — they all tried to follow an agenda of peace. One could say that peace had become a Nordic mentality, deeply rooted among the people. Peace negotiations, both formal, diplomatic sessions and informal get-togethers, have a long tradition in governments, foreign offices, and churches. The Oslo agreement between the leadership of the Palestinians and the Israeli government resulted in a diplomatic breakthrough, although not in lasting peace. Norway has led many such diplomatic ventures in many hot spots. The church agencies have more and more been involved in and given support to peace endeavors in many places around the globe, for instance, Ethiopia, Sudan, Liberia, Colombia, Sri Lanka, and Central America, just to mention a few examples. As a result of the Life and Peace conference, an international Life and Peace Institute for action research on conflict resolution was initiated. Although international in character, its major donors are Nordic. They have produced many studies on the role of religion in conflicts. They have also participated in and developed new methods for conflict resolution in Somalia and Ethiopia.

As the nuclear conflict subsided after the fall of the socialist states around 1990, other conflicts came to the surface in Africa and in Yugoslavia. They were conflicts of another nature. The Nordic countries and churches have to a large extent maintained a high profile in the conflict resolution mechanisms applied. The twinning of churches of the South with counterparts in the North has developed new links. Many people at the grass roots are concerned and involved in conflicts far away. This is a concrete result of the agenda of peace, justice, and integrity of creation. As we have seen, the peace issue was a priority for a few church leaders before the Second World War. It continued after the war with efforts for reconstruction and reconciliation. At the end of the century minds turned to other parts of the world, where the same agenda with new methods was pursued.

Since 1870 Finland has had special links to northern Namibia, formerly Deutsche Südwestafrika, through the Finnish Missionary Society. A folk church was built up by missionaries among the Ovambo and Kavango people, bordering Angola. It is the only country outside northern Europe where the majority of the population is Lutheran. Many participants of the liberation movement were children of the church. In its struggle for independence Namibia's people and church stood together. Much support has been given to Namibia during this struggle, and special links developed between the first Namibian bishops, Leonard Auala and Kleopas Dumeni, and Finland. For the Nordic churches it was of utmost importance to support their struggle for liberation.

Globalization reached the Nordic churches rapidly toward the end of the millennium. Churches of the South have come much closer. The Nordic churches are part of the worldwide church. The quest for peace and justice has been in the forefront in this development. So it was also in the days of Saint Augustine. Most remarkable in the ecumenical world was the Second Vatican Council, 1962-65. This is treated in chapter 8. Although there are major differences between the Lutheran churches and the Vatican on doctrine and in tradition, the exchange on issues of justice and peace is massive compared to the 1950s. Nordic bishops are invited to participate in services in Rome and even attend the bishops' conference of the Roman Catholic Church in the Vatican. Ecumenically, some are disappointed that the opening of Vatican II has not accelerated at a faster speed. Others look realistically at the ecumenical map and discover that many things have happened since Vatican II. A major event was the celebration of Saint Birgitta in 2003, mainly at her own church in Vadstena, but also in many places connected to her in Sweden and Finland and throughout Europe.

Another major breakthrough has taken place in relation to the European Union (EU). Denmark had been a member of the European Economic Community since 1972. Finland and Sweden joined in 1992 after the fall of the Soviet Union and in the midst of internal economic crises. Norway and Iceland have chosen to stay outside membership but are associated with the European Exchange System. While most countries of central and eastern Europe had joined the EU by 2004, a new political reality is there. Although the Nordic countries and the Nordic folk churches may have marginal effects on the EU, they will have more effect on the cooperation among the countries around the Baltic Sea, which have been separated through most of the twentieth century. New ventures are opening up. A theological exchange is taking place, called TheoBalt. Many of the churches around the Baltic Sea are participating in these theological conferences. Also, the Porvoo Agreement, signed by many Lutheran churches around the Baltic Sea as well as the Anglican churches of the British Isles, is a good foundation for practical exchange of church personnel and cooperation at large. Other aspects of the Porvoo Agreement are dealt with in chapter 8.

What about the relation to the German churches? As we saw earlier, the ties were strong immediately following World War II. After almost half a century of limited contacts to Germany because of the heavy influence of American and Anglo-Saxon culture through language and media, the contacts are now increasing thanks to Germany now having a single capital, Berlin, and to the cooperation around the Baltic Sea. The five Nordic folk churches have signed formal agreements of practical cooperation with the Evangelische Kirche in Deutschland.

The ecumenical relations developed since World War II have truly changed the Nordic folk churches. These churches have been active in developing the instruments for ecumenism. They have also been challenged to change their ways by ecumenical partners in the South. Thousands of individuals have had their lives changed in their encounters with ecumenical partners in meetings, in conferences, or as voluntary workers. The *oikoumene* came to stay as the world got smaller in the twentieth century.

7. Church and Society

PETER LODBERG AND BJÖRN RYMAN

The Welfare State

The development of the Nordic societies after World War II has concentrated around the welfare state. It is based on economic growth, industrialization, and growth in population. At the same time, in all countries people moved from the country to the cities. New suburbs were established and church life had to adjust to the suburban style of life. As an immediate effect of the new structure of society, many new churches were built and the tradition of church architecture was renewed with the inspiration from functionalism and modernism. In this chapter the process of the Nordic folk churches' adjustment to the new society after World War II will be analyzed.

In most European countries the old system of state churches was abolished around the year 1900 or after World War I. This was not the case in the Nordic countries. They were ethnically, culturally, and religiously homogeneous countries and held on to the Lutheran state churches as they were known from the Reformation. The close ties between church, state, nation, and people were strengthened during World War II. There was a need for national identity, and the folk churches were able to play an important role as a moral force against the German occupation. The leaders of the Nordic folk churches held high expectations

99

that the churches could continue to serve as a rallying point for the nations after the war, but in most cases they were disappointed.

According to church law, the Nordic folk churches built upon the classical Lutheran understanding of the difference between *jus in sacris* and *jus circa sacra*, which means that the state is responsible for external issues such as church law, finances, organization, and administration, while the inner issues related to liturgy, church books, etc., are taken care of by the churches themselves. But these latter issues were also part of the prerogative of the state, and in most cases the head of state, e.g., the king or queen, had to approve new liturgies, new hymnbooks, or new Bible translations to be used in worship. In most Nordic countries new church structures were established in the aftermath of World War II, but close links to the traditional way of organizing the churches were maintained. Evolution instead of revolution in church structures and church life became a fact, which characterizes the developments in all Nordic countries.

As already mentioned, the movement of people from country to city because of industrialization was important to the churches. In Sweden the population growth from 1945 to 1965 was from 6.6 million to 8 million. In 1945, 3.9 million lived in villages in the country and 2.8 million in the cities. Twenty-five years later, in 1970, the figures were reversed: 3.5 million were living in the country while 4.5 million were in the cities. The picture was the same in the other Nordic countries. The changes reflect a new composition of the working force. In 1945, 25 percent of the Swedish people were linked to farming, 43 percent to industrial production, 23 percent to trade, and 10 percent to the public sector. In 1970, 8 percent of the population was linked to farming and 20 percent to the public sector, with the rest divided between industrial production and trade. This picture is also common to all Nordic countries as a consequence of the establishment of the welfare state. It was financed by the tax system and created a big public sector with a high degree of social security for its citizens.

In the immediate aftermath of World War II there was a movement of people among the Nordic countries. The agricultural crisis in Finland led many Finns to move to Sweden to find work. But also, immigration from Italy, Hungary, Greece, and Yugoslavia to especially Sweden and Denmark was significant. In 1970, 11 percent of the Swedish population was born outside Sweden. This can be compared to Denmark's 6 percent, Norway's 5.8 percent, and Finland's 2.3 percent. Slowly but certainly, the homogeneous Nordic countries began a process of becoming more multicultural and thus also multireligious societies. Especially with the influx of refugees from Asia and the Middle East in the 1980s and 1990s, this development continues.

Compared to the rest of Europe, it is interesting that all Nordic countries after World War II embarked on the way to the social welfare state. It is often maintained that this development has much to do with the existence of big Lutheran national folk churches in all countries. The former chairman of the Danish parliament, Erling Olsen, said the very idea of the social welfare state is the secularized idea of "love your neighbor" in Christianity. This idea is shared by all political parties and organizations in civic society, because they all are part of the same Protestant history with its work ethic and positive understanding of the need for a strong and centralized structure in society. At the same time, people accept the tax system and its distribution of welfare.

Common to most Nordic countries was the role of the Social Democratic Parties in establishing the welfare state. It was done in different ways according to the special contexts in the different countries, but seen from outside, the developments were similar. In Sweden the idea was to regard society as the good and safe home for everybody. This vision points to the importance of the national fellowship and the classless society. It is the responsibility of the society to take care of the people and secure safety and comfort for all citizens. The Swedish model with its strong policy on social issues and a big public sector was an inspiration for Social Democratic governments in Norway and Denmark. In all three countries these governments were in power for most of the time between 1945 and 2000, which gave continuity to the vision and its realization.

The model of the welfare state worked because it produced "progress," wealth, and centralized authority. The period from 1945 to 1970 was characterized by very strong economic growth. The gross national product grew by more than 5 percent per year. Room was made for new initiatives and experiments in social services, school systems, and communication. Private income and consumption grew at an enormous speed, which created an optimistic attitude toward material progress. Developments in technology based on new scientific knowledge and administered in a rationalistic manner were supposed to create equal and good conditions for everybody. The basic idea behind the welfare system was to give everyone a fair chance to succeed in life, and the architects of the welfare state were convinced that everybody could get a happy life if equal conditions were provided by the state. And most importantly, every citizen had a right to the opportunity to succeed despite differences in class and family background. It was the duty of the state to secure that this personal right was respected and nurtured.

Society was seen as a technological enterprise. The politicians and civil servants were the engineers of society, and the human being was considered a rational person that behaved according to rational choices. To map the attitude and behavior of people the whole area of social sciences was developed. Political and economical sciences were also developed as a necessary tool to predict and plan the future of society on the basis of the human being as a rational entrepreneur in the new grand design of the welfare state. Especially in the 1960s and 1970s Marxist ideology and historical materialism were taught at universities and in higher education as the most progressive understanding of the rationality of person and society. From 1989 on, because of the fundamental political and economic changes in Eastern Europe, liberalism took over as the most prominent ideology in society. It remains to be seen if this will change the welfare society fundamentally.

The establishment of the welfare state changed the role and pattern of the family. Education of women and the presence of women in the labor force were carried forward by the feminist movement. Equality among men and women became an important political issue. Free abortion and the right of women to decide for themselves divided people and families along new lines. In Denmark, Christians from conservative low-church pietistic and Roman Catholic groups came together and established the Christian People's Party in 1970 as a protest against the law on free abortion from the same year. In Norway the bishop of Borg, Per Lønning, resigned in 1975 because of the law on free abortion. Also in Norway, the Christian People's Party voted against this law.

In all Nordic countries Christian parties have taken part in the political life. Most influential has been the Christian People's Party in Norway. It has carried the most votes and taken part in several governments, and the leader has served as prime minister. In Sweden and Finland the Christian parties have gained about 10 percent of the vote in some elections. The Danish Christian Party has always been very small. It has been severely criticized in church circles for mixing politics and Christianity and for being too conservative on ethical questions and family values. The Oslo bishop Eivind Berggrav formulated a similar criticism of the Norwegian Christian People's Party in 1950. He said the party mixed the confession of the Christian creed with party politics. This made a new law out of the gospel. It would limit the Christian message to a small sector of society. Berggrav also found that Christian freedom was at stake if the political goal was to be understood as the realization of God's intentions for society through the work of a special political party. Obviously, Berggrav wanted to keep an open space for a dialogue with the Social Democratic Party even though he disagreed with its policy on certain matters.

In Denmark the most influential minister of church affairs was Mrs. Bodil Koch from the Social Democratic Party. (See the biographical sketch of Mrs. Koch in chapter 9.) She held a master's degree in theology and was married to Professor Hal Koch, a very influential church historian at the University of Copenhagen and well known to the Danish public. Bodil Koch was minister from 1953 to 1966, during which time secularization took place, the welfare state was established, and Denmark was integrated into NATO during the Cold War.

Bodil Koch formulated a new Social Democratic church policy, which finally broke with the old idea of separation between state and church. An important aspect was the many new members of the congregation councils around the country from the Social Democratic Party. Their presence ensured that the church was a spiritual reality and remained the church of the people. To Bodil Koch the folk church was both part of the official state structure and the church of Christ in Denmark as formed through the centuries. She took the initiative to set up a commission to look into the structure of the Danish folk church in a modern society. The commission worked from 1964 to 1971 and formulated a number of proposals, which have been discussed and implemented in the period up to 1993. Among the proposals were a new structure for the ecumenical work of the folk church and the establishment of both new clergy positions for students and different public institutions. The commission did not touch upon the relationship between state and church. This might be an important issue for a new commission in the future.

The relationship between state and church came up as an important issue in the other Nordic countries as well. In Finland the church was able to control the discussion because it framed the issue, and the relationship between state and church was maintained despite the policy of many left-wing politicians. In Sweden a long process finally led to the separation of state and church in 2000. The Church of Norway has retained both its close relationship with the state and the freedom to take actions when agreed upon by the General Church Assembly. All Nordic folk churches except for the Danish one have established a structure and practice that allows them to speak on behalf of the church in matters of serious concern. In Denmark, where the folk church does not have an assembly or council, church matters are taken care of by the Parliament and the minister of church affairs. The bishops of the Danish folk church meet on a regular basis, but they seldom take common actions or issue common statements. This is one reason why the Danish folk church has had great difficulty participating in the ecumenical movement and agreeing on joint declarations like Porvoo, Leuenberg, or Charta Oecumenica.

The adjustment of the Nordic folk churches to the welfare state had important consequences for the ordination of women. In all Nordic countries the state saw the ordination of women as a practical question related to the general rules on the labor market and the equality between men and women. The debate around female ordination was heated in most countries, partly because it was seen as the state's intervention into the inner life of the church and partly because the majority of bishops and clergy in the beginning were against ordaining women for biblical and theological reasons. The first women ordained were in Denmark, in 1947. In Iceland the first woman was ordained in 1974. This happened almost without discussion. The candidate had several times without success applied for a position as clergy but had never been called by any congregation before 1974. In Norway female ordination took place in 1961. It was welcomed by liberal groups and feminist activists, but was very much criticized by conservative Christians despite the fact that all regulations had been followed and no male candidate had wanted to serve in the concerned parish. In Sweden the General Assembly of the Swedish Church accepted a new church law that allowed the ordination of women. It was used in 1960 when the first three female clergy were ordained — one by the archbishop, Gunnar Hultgren. The debate in Sweden was fueled by a declaration by biblical scholars at the theological faculties in Lund and Uppsala in 1951. They argued that there is no biblical background for the ordination of women. Despite this and similar opposition, the number of female pastors has increased in all Nordic folk churches since 1980, and the first female bishops have now been elected in Sweden, Norway, and Denmark.

It is important to note that the ecumenical discussion on the ministry in the Lutheran World Federation (LWF) and the World Council of Churches (WCC) has played a marginal role in the Nordic debate. It was carried forward by the state together with very small groups and individuals inside the folk churches. Theological issues have played a minor role compared to the issue of human rights and equality between male and female in a growing labor market.

Social Ethics

A tremendous change has taken place in the Nordic countries regarding social ethics. The churches were once seen as the pillars of morality in society. The Ten Commandments had been taught to every generation both in school and in confirmation classes. Most people regarded the

Sermon on the Mount as the highest set of ideals to live by. School in-struction was based on these teachings. The old, close connection be-tween church and society showed itself best preserved through the schools. At the time of the Second World War most schools in the Nordic countries had morning prayers and confessional religious in-struction in a subject called Christendom. This monolithic and self-evident world crumbled, at different speeds and with different intensity in each Nordic country, based on the resolution of the different Social Democratic governments.

Of course, both church and society could be accused of double stan-dards. Teaching and preaching is one thing, living and practicing an-other. Until the 1960s the adherents of the traditional revival movements joined with bishops and clergy in upholding what they considered Christian values in society, be it in schools, in culture, or in mass media. Loud protests sounded when authors and film producers delved into what was considered taboo in private morality, particularly in sexual af-fairs. Some authors felt that censorship was hanging over them. In the 1940s and 1950s there were many heated debates when books and films portrayed a realism not previously presented publicly.

As a matter of fact, the Nordic countries have a long tradition of freedom of press and speech. The laws for Sweden and Finland date back to 1766. The freedom of printing was part of the constitution. However, in religious matters there was regulation and censorship. As in most Western countries, the limits for cultural creativity were challenged rad-ically in the 1960s when suddenly everything seemed to be allowed in print and on film. A wave of commercial pornography swept through the Nordic countries. The protests came mainly from what were consid-ered conservative Christians, and they were marginalized by public opinion.

Most bishops in the Nordic countries lived in a culturally conserva-tive environment based on traditional Christian values both in private and public life. Several of them were strong personalities. The growing liberalism among the cultural elite was grateful to find in them a target for their arrows. A good example is Yngve Brilioth, archbishop in Swe-den from 1950 to 1958. He had served as professor and bishop in southern Sweden and supported public protests against what was considered immorality. In his pastoral letter in 1950 he defended his cultural conservatism, stressing the ties between church and school and upholding a traditional Christian morality against the new ideas of sexual education in the schools. He saw himself sharing the same views as Nathan Söderblom, his father-in-law. These views were scorned by liberal newspapers and tabloids, which sold well in those days. To the public at large, bishops and clergy had lost their authority to advise on private morality. This loss of authority occurred in all Nordic countries in the 1950s and 1960s.

The heated debate on faith and scientific knowledge in Sweden around 1950 had enormous repercussions. Bishops and professors stood in the forefront defending Christian faith in those days. As this was a media event, which no one had anticipated, it ran its own course. The largest and most influential daily newspaper in Sweden painted the advocates of the church as out-of-date, and they looked somewhat bewildered. Half a century later philosophers and historians have concluded that the bishops and professors performed quite well with their arguments, and there was no reason to ridicule them. Seen in a historical perspective, the monopoly of the church on matters of faith and morality was challenged. The debate heralded a new age of rationalism. The new elite was branded as cultural radicals, and it comprised a network of intellectuals, publishers, academics, and leading educators. They were present in all Nordic countries, and their influence was felt in the academic and cultural world.

In Norway this group of intellectuals had a definite program, which in many ways made common cause with the Social Democratic Party in its hard-line push for a monolithic welfare state. Its most ardent opponent was Bishop Berggrav. He was afraid of the strong state and said no to all tendencies of a monopolized welfare society.

Berggrav's view of church and society was to a large extent shared by other bishops in the Nordic countries. This is particularly true of the leader of the young church movement in Sweden, Manfred Björkquist. In their efforts to further the motto "The people of Sweden — a people of God," the leaders of this group were considered culturally conservative, even reactionary, by leading Social Democrats. As both Berggrav and Björkquist were outstanding speakers and communicators, they spread fear right up to the top of Social Democratic leadership. The Swedish prime minister wrote in his diary, released fifty years later, that despite Björkquist's talk of humanism and dialogue, in his heart he was a reactionary and as a politician would have been "our greatest enemy." Lately it has been revealed that Berggrav had plans to start a political party along these lines. Berggrav, Björkquist, Brilioth — these men considered themselves heirs to Söderblom whose personal ambition was to be like him as church leaders. It is one of the paradoxes in history that the high esteem in which these bishops were held during the tough war years was worth very little in the postwar period when a new society was built by politicians and social engineers. The role of the church in building a society based on Christian values that would influence literature, press, radio, film, and schools was minimized. The bishops had imagined the postwar period as a flourishing age for the churches as folk churches, as a chance for the churches to be what they were meant to be for the people.

These strong bishops whose ideals of life were shaped at the turn of the century were not appreciated by a new generation with more secularized ideas for shaping a new society. They were formed by a male society, particularly in the authoritarian and disciplined environment of university theology and clergy. They employed immense self-discipline in private life and as public figures. Their working capacity both in producing books, articles, and sermons and as administrators of church and society at large was enormous. Some were wholehearted fighters for the ideas they believed in. They were admired by their adherents and were good at raising funds for the projects they believed in. Their greatest emphasis was on personality and character development. If an individual received these ideals, a Christian personality would develop that in turn would form a better society. Their ideals were to a large extent male in character. Of strong character, self-disciplined, hardworking, obedient to superiors and leaders for their flock — so they saw themselves and trained others to be. The young church movement in both Sweden and Finland later encompassed these male ideas. In Finland they were spearheaded by the clergy serving in the front line during the war. Teachers and doctors who had the greatest influence in decisions of upbringing and in setting standards of sexual morals were to a great extent in congruence with the ideals of the church.

People brought up in the revival movements supported the bishops in this context, although they might not share the theological and ecclesiological standpoint of the hierarchy. Where the revival movements had greatest success in numbers, Norway and Finland, there was also the greatest support for traditional Christian values in society. While changes in attitudes were slower in Norway and Finland, they happened at a faster pace in Sweden and Denmark. Most people agree that the lasting results of the revival movements were the social ethics they instilled in society. But as their theological heritage was one of conversion, biblicism, and individual ethics, they lacked a coherent view of social ethics for all of society.

In building strong welfare societies, politicians, clergy, and people were initially of the same mind in their quest for sound and healthy people. Doctors and nurses played important roles in implanting a healthy lifestyle, including high standards of behavior in matters of reproduction. The so-called people's movements, including sports associations and youth clubs like the YMCA and YWCA, were favored by society for their roles in character and personality development. These voluntary associations flourished prior to and after the world war. They were regarded as the backbone for a healthy society. In the upbringing of young people there was cooperation between voluntary organizations and the architects of the welfare state. The type of character development wanted was collective in nature. Individualism was not a goal per se. Athletic camps could in the 1950s start with compulsory morning prayers. Amateur sports were much favored by society, particularly for boys. Girls tended to favor gymnastics, swimming, and riding. Soccer and marathon running for women were unheard of. The feminization of traditional male sports came in the 1980s. Professional sports were more or less forbidden or not on the agenda in the Nordic countries. All Nordic nations were successful in the Olympic Games after the war. Sweden, undamaged by the war, was the best nation in the 1948 Games in London. In 1952 Norway hosted the Winter Olympics and Finland the Summer Games.

For these war-torn countries these major events marked the end of the postwar period. This amateur world of sports before television networks were established was gradually to vanish. A new individualism, even in a team sport like soccer, was more attractive than old-time collectivism. Professionalism took over many sports as television and commercialism walked hand in hand into the affluent society.

In the sense of character building of the nations, church and society were more or less one until the 1960s. The youth organizations of the folk churches were quite strong after the war. They adjusted to the modernization process and recruited many members. The Christian student movements were also active and had many members from all faculties, although the theological faculties dominated. In some places they were divided on the issues of high-church liturgy or low-church practice. Confessionalism and liturgical practice tended to split the movement. In Sweden it had three different branches: the free churches, the folk church, and the evangelical churches. As a more affluent and materialistic society developed, students searched for Christian transcendental answers beyond or maybe in conflict with modern liberal developments.

From the 1950s onward things changed at a fast pace. The pace was fastest in Sweden, followed by Denmark, with Finland and Norway lagging behind. The half-century just passed has probably produced more shifts in people's intrinsic values than the last half-millennium. At the time of the Reformation it took at least a generation to change value patterns. Many observers are baffled at the speed in modern society at which age-old traditional values were transcended. This is mainly true of morals concerning sexual reproduction and the roles of the sexes. The debate had started already in the 1930s, and it concerned both the low birthrate and individual freedom concerning sexuality. At that time church and society were almost unanimous in trying to prevent premarital sexual relations as well as abortions. At the same time, there were sterilization programs, particularly for young women who by society were condemned not to be able to fulfill their tasks as mothers. This has been severely criticized by posterity for its socio-racial bias, and surviving victims have been given token compensation. The folk churches were part of society and did not protest against this legislation on normal human rights grounds.

As in all developments, artists are the first to break cultural and moral taboos. Authors in all countries wrote more daring and realistic novels during these years. In Norway there was a court case about censorship of a novel. In Sweden more and more films were produced that broke the set pattern. In the 1950s Ingmar Bergman had his breakthrough as a film director. He dealt with rational modern man's existential dilemma without the presence of a benevolent, gracious God. One of his first low-budget black-and-white movies, *The Seventh Seal*, dealt with the anguish of death. Set against the backdrop of the Black Death, circa 1350, his alter ego, the Christian crusader returning home from the Holy Land, is confronted with the inevitable result of the plague: death for him, his family, and companions. It occurs when the seventh seal of the book of Revelation is broken. Bergman was hailed as a great producer when this film appeared in 1957. Also, people from the folk church saw in his films the existential questions dealt with in a new dramatic way. As a son of a vicar, he struggled with himself in condemning a too strong paternalistic authority. As his succeeding films in the 1960s dealt with similar issues, like the silence of God, but through shocking scenes, many traditionalists reacted and protested. This contributed to a sharp controversy in the mid-1960s whether traditional Christian values should be the basis of society or not. Particularly Sweden was in the 1960s portrayed as a nation of license and sin. The fever of this debate rose dramatically around 1968.

Up until 1968 there had been pro and con debates on ethics in society. The uniform model of church and society together was more or less broken in most of the Nordic churches. A freer form of upbringing and more allowance for sexual liberty spread, particularly in the big cities. As part of the basic school curriculum, education in sexual relations was introduced at the time much of the school system was going through big changes. Everything in society seemed to be made anew, particularly for the young generation. Antiauthoritarian and antipaternalistic with a great love for self-indulgence, a new student generation was ripe for the youth revolt that hit Europe in May 1968. To a certain extent it set the agenda for society and also the churches.

The 1968 revolt had many consequences, although most of them were short-lived. Some would have come anyway, but events made them come faster. In addition to the sexual revolution and antiauthoritarianism already mentioned, other aspects were feminism and gender awareness, anti-Americanism through protests against the Vietnam War and the capitalist multinational companies and the banks, anticolonialism and antiracism through support of liberation movements in the Third World, and a prosocialist support in the nuclear arms race. These issues were also present when the WCC held its general assembly in Uppsala in 1968. For the Nordic churches the icon of "1968" is double in size: the general youth protest and the protest events at Uppsala.

For the churches the issues of peace and justice were put at the forefront in a new way. Peace and justice issues were nothing new to the ecumenical movement. What was new was the aggressive mood in which they were tackled. The rich industrial world, beginning with America but also including the Nordic countries, was put on trial for the war in Vietnam and for its capitalist exploitation of small poor countries. Close to revolutionary calls were heard. By outsiders in the establishment and by traditionalists in the revival movements these cries were heard as a new unbiblical age. Others in the ecumenical movement heard them as a prophetic summons against injustice and violations of the biblical shalom. Different interpretations of the Bible were used. To the traditional Lutheran theology there came a new impetus of social ethics. It split the churches. Some said the church was politicized along socialist and revolutionary lines. Others accused the churches of having stood on the side of the oppressors and fit their Bible interpretation accordingly. As the cultural revolution in China happened during these years and Mao's little red book was translated, some of the avant-garde were regarded as Maoists.

As this movement of protest for peace and social justice permeated many parts of the world and particularly the churches involved in the ecumenical movement, we will portray only some of the characteristics for the Nordic churches. Even the Second Vatican Council, 1962-65, and its implementation were part of this mood of renewal. To Pope John XXIII an aggiornamento was necessary, to get the church up to date on the affairs of this world. This attitude affected many at the

Uppsala '68 Assembly as well. Paradoxically, the opening of the Catholic Church to other churches and to new solutions on social issues made the Lutheran Nordic folk churches open up to Catholicism more than they had in four hundred years. At the same time, there was both revolution in the air and a new approach to Catholic liturgy and hierarchy. The revolutionary fervor of the 1968 happenings did not follow one single pattern, but different threads entangled into each other.

Most of the controversies have arisen over the political agenda of those considered revolutionaries of the day. The loudest protests were against the United States and its war in Vietnam. This movement for the freedom of the Vietnamese to decide their own future was very strong in the Nordic countries. It carried the day in public opinion, and also in the ecumenical movement. Olof Palme was the most outstanding politician on this side of the debate. In its wake followed anti-American feelings of differing strengths in the Nordic countries. Did this automatically mean that the protesters supported the Soviet Union and China? It is true that the study of Marxism had never been so intense as in the 1970s. In many university subjects it was part of the agenda. Due to the new interest in Latin American liberation theology and the pedagogy of liberation, presented by Paulo Freire, the Marxist interpretation of society made its way also into theological teaching. This was done from the perspective of the poor. This analysis through the dependence school in economics had an impact on those dealing with the development of the Third World. The Marxist analysis used was more geared against capitalism and against exploitation of Third World countries than for support for the Soviet Union and China. The Chinese model of development was considered by some to be superior to others that were more democratic and capitalist, like the Indian model. Chinese development deliberately stressed the masses doing things together, obliterating individualism and self-interest. Some intellectuals of these days, although a small minority, including clergy, were proponents of this type of culture revolution. To their dismay the revolution never happened. The world went in another direction.

One of the legacies of these events for the Nordic churches was a commitment to the struggle of the poor nations and churches. There had been something of a revival for development aid in all Nordic countries, with strong institutionalized aid and development agencies. The aid to Biafra happened at this time in 1968-69, and television coverage had a spin-off effect. Both traditionalists and leftists joined hands in the development project. They disagreed on methods but cooperated on the goal of justice and equality for all people. While the new tune of 1968 was advocacy on behalf of the voiceless, traditional churchgoers did not disagree but continued to support programs for better quality of life for all. This congruence-instead-of-conflict made the development lobby strong in all the Nordic countries.

Another legacy is that social ethics took the place of individual ethics. Constructed evil replaced personal evil. The Lutheran doctrine of the two kingdoms had been questioned since the 1930s when the totalitarian states were dominating. A new reforming theology evolved, partly inspired by liberation theology. It stressed the structural change of society more than individual conversion. As the rich, exploiting societies had to change, including the affluent Nordic states, the right place to start was in the center of exploitation. A favorite target was transnational corporations and their trade patterns. Another was the profit made by most private companies. Most contempt was poured on the armament industry, particularly when exporting weapons. There were many such campaigns in the 1970s and 1980s in most industrial societies. These social ethics played a role in the Nordic countries in establishing a code of conduct for the companies, and helped governments to a certain consciousness when regulating these areas.

The theology of the two kingdoms with its tendency to isolate Christian living and thinking was replaced with a theology concerned with society and not afraid of mixing into big politics. The biblical shalom is a matter not just of peace between humans, but of peace for all humanity. Justice was interpreted as social justice and not only a just relationship between God and man. Without social justice there could be no peace. In the same way sin was not considered a personal error to be corrected and forgiven, but institutionalized, superindividual systems that imprison people. The rich world was also accused of sins of omission in not seeing the plight of the poor and the suffering of racist regimes. God's will was relevant in all of society and not just in the inner world of the pious Christian. The world here and now wrote the agenda for the committed Christian.

Was this theology ever applied or was it just discussed at coffee breaks? For many in the Christian youth movements it was essential; many members were to a great extent shaped by these ideals. The struggle for justice; for economic, social, and gender equality; and for a greener environment was at the top of the agenda. The creation as a God-given gift had always been there in theology, but now it received new impetus. Apart from protests against environmentally unsound practices, new church services were created. They took their inspiration from the Old Testament, particularly the Psalms and the Jubilee Year. A simple life-style combined with a global consciousness of the limited resources on our planet made this movement very strong. Several of the bishops at the turn of the millennium drew inspiration from this movement. Their sermons and actions showed this. They wrote letters and signed manifestos in solidarity with creation. On the practical level, more and more of the parishes created environmental plans for all their actions. As many of them owned forests, there was a concerted effort to take care of them in a sound way and preserve the endangered species and not just think how profitable they might be. The funeral system and the upkeep of the churches were adjusted to an environmentally sound sustainability. In much of this, church and society went in the same direction. Most people realized that the postwar economic boom had caused great damage to nature. To restore nature and liberate it from toxin was a long and expensive process. Sins against creation could not just be forgiven. They had to be put right. A theology of stewardship developed with an emphasis on responsibility for God's creation.

The 1968 events also had an impact on family values, cohabitation, and partnership. The common understanding between church and society up until then was that family life was very important for all members of society. The Nordic countries are in the long run not very different in this aspect from most industrialized and modern societies. The difference might be that they seemed to be ahead of many other countries and that much publicity was focused on the sexual freedom in some Nordic countries in the 1950s and 1960s. Up until the 1970s bishops, clergy, and traditionalists from revival movements and virtually all the free churches protested against the liberal trends in society, where premarital sexual relations were being accepted as a custom. Cohabitation without wedding and formal marriage became common. New liberal abortion laws were legislated by parliaments in all the Nordic countries. Most controversy and protest appeared in Norway. Denmark and Sweden were more liberal. New networks of women's liberation groups were formed with radical demands on legislation. This happened at a very fast pace, so fast that many feared it would accelerate even more swiftly.

On the one hand there was the motto of equal rights, which was worldwide at this time. Equality was the political slogan for a decade, particularly for the leftist parties in the Nordic countries. This was meant for political offices and employment opportunities, but also between the sexes. Women's representation at all levels of decision making increased considerably from the 1960s onward. Norway took the lead by electing a majority of women to Parliament and also to government. Gro Harlem Brundtland was a successful prime minister and a clear sign of this progress. At the millennium women held approximately half the seats in the different Nordic parliaments and in the cabinets of each country. Equal opportunity has always been there, but the political push to make equality a reality in decision making came in the 1970s. So it was for the decision-making bodies of the churches as well. Local church councils and national bodies saw an influx of women from the 1980s on. With some delay the churches here followed the political trend of society.

Economic equality among the citizens has been a vision for many in the Nordic countries. This vision came closest to reality in the 1970s. Solidarity was a key word in those days. Taxation reached a peak around 1980. There was a movement among concerned people to abstain from higher salaries in order to benefit the lowly paid in their own country, and in the end the poor in the Third World. Clergy with much academic distinction, for instance, abstained from salary raises during these years of high inflation. The ratio between the highest paid and the lowest paid in an office or in a firm was not very big after taxes had been paid. It was traditionally lowest in Norway.

Women moving into the job market went into the public sector, which grew immensely, requiring high taxes. The caring sector of society — children, elderly, education — became a world of women. Wages did not rise to what they expected. Taxes had reached a ceiling. The crisis for the fully built-up welfare state was a fact around 1990. Economically, it could not bear its own burden. A political, economic, and social change was inevitable in all countries. The already lowly paid became unemployed. The able-bodied had to work harder under more stress. They were burned-out. The state health insurance expenses skyrocketed. Everybody was bewildered.

Norway and Denmark managed this crisis best. Finland reached a high unemployment rate, although state finances were in good shape. The blow for Sweden was that its ideal of a good society for all was crushed in the global economy. Solidarity had to yield to efficiency of the market. As more and more people got sick or burned out, doctors, psychologists, and others tried to offer cures and answers. A new demand was put to the churches. What is important in life? All those days of stress — was that life? Lectures and literature on the meaning of life from clergy and theologians were produced as never before. The churches did have something to contribute that the people wanted. On the other hand, was it just ordinary therapeutic conversation? Or did the church in its teaching have something to say about purpose in life, how to "love thy neighbor," about sound work ethics and Luther's teachings on the calling for everybody? The question remains, as this is an ongoing process. What is the best way to rescue the general welfare policy to reach equality for all in a civil society? All grapple with these issues. The bishops in Finland issued strong statements and called for solidarity with those who were forced to go to soup kitchens. In all the Nordic countries the bishops have been strong defenders of the solidarity behind the welfare state.

The services of the folk churches are asked for in times of crisis. When accidents, murders, and traumas happen with great media coverage, a crisis center is established locally. Often the church or its ministers come into focus. The good society was little prepared when unexplained disasters or tragedies occurred. Without asking for it, the church was in the center. Tragic, unexplainable death did not fit into the good society consisting of good people in a sound environment. Evil as a force in society had to be tackled in a realistic, existential way. If a national trauma occurs, mass media quickly turn to bishops and clergy to explain the unexplainable.

The existence of evil in society and in human beings was not on the agenda during the height of the welfare state. It was thought good children would continue as model citizens as long as the conditions in society were good. As young adults turn to crime, join criminal motorbike gangs, or become neo-Nazi racist skinheads, ordinary citizens gasp. How can this development take place? This was not the intention. An awakening to a more realistic view of the presence of evil in human nature and in society is slowly coming. The folk churches and their theologians have a contribution to make in grasping and explaining evil occurrences in society.

At the millennium the image of church and society was different than it was fifty or sixty years earlier. Around 1950, society was going to marginalize the church. Elected politicians and enlightened citizens were going to set the agenda for creating a good society for all. In many ways the welfare state managed to create good conditions for most of its citizens. Even in the welfare state the family was considered the nucleus of society at large. Many of the first reforms favored the family as a unit: better urban housing and planning, child allowances, maternal leave, longer vacations, a school system fit for everybody, a society also including the disadvantaged and those with different abilities. This inclusiveness meant that the strong social state became centralized. Without this concentration of resources and decision making, the welfare state for all would not function. When the welfare state had been extended to most walks of life, the rights of each individual were set at the center. These rights were protected, and a new individualism took hold in the fully built-up welfare state. The affluent society could afford to give multiple choice to each individual, as nobody would risk falling through the social web. This new individualism tended to abandon old collective models of common solidarity. It demanded both the economic, social, and educational benefits of the social welfare state and at the same time the right of each individual to do his or her own thing. This new form of individualism made common cause with the new feminism emerging around 1968 and other antiauthoritarian and antipatriarchal patterns.

The new individualism became opposed to the traditional family as an economic and social unit in society. New customs developed. Up until 1970 the nuclear family had been the model for society and its legislation. At different rates in different countries, the strength of the family as the natural unit decreased. Some politicians launched the slogan "Smash the family," meaning the traditional family patterns. Some justified this because much violence and oppression was wreaked upon wives and children by abusing fathers. Others wanted more liberty for the partners to choose new lifestyles and not to be locked into confining patterns. Tax legislation no longer favored the family as a unit. Women's rights movements and feminist theology welcomed this development.

At the same time, cohabitation became a new form of family formation. Church weddings decreased, although they never sank below 60 percent. Compared to other Western countries, birthrates have been fairly consistent with a slow increase of population. On the other hand, abortion rates have been high, although not as high as in other countries.

There has been much protest against this development. It has mainly come from traditional Christians in mainline folk churches, but more vehemently from revival movements and from Roman Catholic and Orthodox Christians. They argue that the Nordic churches should have protested much more against this secular development. Bishops in the Nordic churches did argue against it and defended traditional family values from a perspective of a theology of creation. The response was mixed and much of it negative. This is one reason for the Christian parties to gain strength, and they were most successful in Norway. On the other hand, traditional everyday parish work was based on traditional family values, favoring special programs for family and children. That has been the signature of normal church work, although the newspaper debates have raged over new and old morality.

As the past millennium drew to a close, the issue of homosexuality and same-sex relations was at the top of the ethical agenda in most countries. In the 1990s the Nordic churches recognized that they did not

understand how homosexuals felt they had been treated. Many committees and study groups met to consider the issue from the perspective of
theology of creation, the biblical expressions on the subject, and the will
of God for the sake of procreation, love, and marriage. Most of these
committees have concluded that mistakes have been made throughout
history, but they are usually divided on guidelines for the future. So were
the Nordic churches.

The Nordic societies have legalized same-sex relations. One of the
outstanding questions was the form of ceremony to establish this relation. Were the churches open to performing legal weddings for same-
sex couples? This issue divided churchgoers along traditional and radical
lines. Theologically the radical line reasoned that Jesus never explicitly
condemned homosexuality like Saint Paul did. He embraced people who
were not accepted in his society: women, children, Samaritans. His love
was all-inclusive and did not exclude people. In his time marriage was a
matter of procreation. In our time it is as much a matter of love.

Traditional theologians and Christians take their arguments from
church tradition and from the Bible. They argue that the Bible in both
the Old and New Testaments is explicit in condemning homosexuality.
No church in history has thought to change this. They also argue from
creation that man and woman were created for each other and for procreation. Therefore traditional marriage is the only accepted way of living together. This line has been called the fundamentalist line, which it
also represents in the true sense of the word. The foundation for members of church and society is traditional marriage and the family. Without this cornerstone, church and society will crumble. Therefore it is not
the will of God to alter this order or to adjust theology to please another
opinion of individualism and indulgence.

In the sixty-year span since the world war, a tremendous shift of
opinion has occurred. Traditional values of church and society have
yielded, through the odyssey of modernization, to postmodernism. The
authority of the churches has eroded, but so has the authority of the
strong, centralized society. A new individualism took the role of the collective solidarity. Church and society still shape people's lives, but now
they must compete with other influences broadcast over global multi-

media available for everybody. Few people today will ask authorities for guidance, whether politicians or clergy.

Since the end of the Second World War the self-evident role of the Nordic churches as authorities in moral and ethical questions has diminished. But to the surprise of the modernizers, their roles have not disappeared. They are asked for in a new way when new ethical issues like bioethics arise. The mystery of Christ and Christianity is there and needs to be explained to each generation. The understanding of Christian love to all is asked for again and again. The twentieth-century scenario of allowing Christianity to fade away in a new rational age did not materialize. Instead, nonrational ways to discover the mystery of Christ and of human beings are sought by people as never before.

8. *Theology and Spirituality*

GUNNAR HEIENE

Background — Theology and Spirituality in the Nordic Countries

Theology and spirituality in the Nordic countries have developed many common traits through the last centuries. A common heritage including strong Lutheran folk churches, orthodox Lutheranism, pietistic revivals, and challenges from secularization and a more pluralistic society has led to the idea of a specific "Nordic" version of Lutheranism and a specific "Nordic" spirituality. Of course, this is true only to a certain extent. A closer view will show many unique traits in each of the Nordic countries. It is thus meaningful to look into the theological and spiritual development within the folk churches after the war to identify both common traits and specific developments.

One common background story in the different churches is the debate between conservative and liberal theology that started in the first decades of the twentieth century. In Norway this controversy even led to the establishment of a new theological faculty in 1908, Menighetsfakultetet (MF), which was seen by many as a more conservative alternative to the theological faculty at the University of Oslo (TF).

Another important background story is the influence from German Lutheranism before the war. Of course, the war led to a reorientation, but in many countries the German influence was still present, at least in the first years after the war. New tendencies, like the Luther renaissance and dialectic theology, were of course recognized in the Nordic countries, although the influence varied. The German influence has gradually weakened since the 1950s, and more and more has been replaced by theological literature from the English-speaking world.

It is also important to take into account the experiences from the war itself. In some countries, like Norway, the war led to much closer cooperation between different theological factions, and the traditional antagonism between conservatives and liberals became much less important than before. The traditional tension between the official church, represented by the bishops and clergy, and the lay Christian movement, based on pietistic ideals, was also less visible during the war. In Finland the war was a strong motivation for unity and helped keep the level of conflict between different theological concepts on a low level. Still, in all Nordic countries the traditional conflicts between different models of theology and spirituality were still latent when the war was ended.

A New Focus on the Church in Nordic Lutheranism

Traditionally, the relationship between theology and the folk churches in the Nordic countries was close, almost symbiotic. Even after 1945 the theological faculties were involved in theological discussions that took place within the folk churches, but at the same time a discussion was held on how to define academic theology and its status within the university institution.

In all Nordic countries the theology accepted within the folk churches shows continuity with the theological models developed during the last part of the nineteenth century and especially during the first decades of the twentieth century. A common trait in the Nordic countries is the discussion between old pietistic theology and a more confessional Lutheran theology. There is also a tendency toward criticism of liberal theology and theological models based on personal experience. Instead of this, a more "objective" understanding of theology was introduced.

Of course, the experience during the war was one of the forces behind this change. The war led to a sharper focus on the church as an institution, on issues like sacraments and ordination. This was a part of the aforementioned objective shift in theology. Partly, this shift was also a result of the influences from German theology, both from the Luther renaissance and from Karl Barth's dialectic theology.

Although there were internal differences and discussions between different theological schools both before and after the war, the Nordic theologians and bishops internationally were supposed to be mostly in agreement with each other. In many respects common traits in a "Nordic" theology were identified, although there are obvious exceptions to this pattern.

In Swedish theology the continuity between prewar and postwar theology is easy to see. The new interest in ecclesiology was a very important trait in Swedish theology, with roots in exegetical and dogmatic research. The new research on Reformation theology was an important factor and led to a stronger emphasis on the common interests in academic theology and church life. A breakthrough for this type of theology was Bo Giertz's book *Kristi kyrka* (The church of Christ), published in 1939, which he wrote as a rural parish pastor. In the following years two books of great importance continued this ecclesiological trend in theology, *En bok om kyrkan* (A book on the church), 1942, and *En bok om kyrkans ämbete* (A book on the ministry of the church), 1951. The so-called Uppsala school in exegesis was another important factor behind this new ecclesiology, with its research on cultic issues and on Jesus as Messiah.

Another main development in Swedish theology was the "Lundensian theology" represented by names like Gustav Aulén, Anders Nygren, and Ragnar Bring. The impulses from leading professors at the theological faculty in Lund on the Swedish clergy were of great importance in the years before and after the war. Nygren's book *Den kristna kärlekstanken genom tiderna — Eros och Agape,* published from 1930 to 1936, is well known as an example of his method of "motif research." The theological faculty in Lund influenced a great part of the Swedish clergy both before and after the war. In his book Nygren presented Christian belief seen from the perspective of a single motif, the agape motif. Aulén had for many years been a professor in systematic theology, until he became bishop of Strängnäs (1933-53). Through his book on the different reconciliation theories *(Christus Victor)* he had influenced many theologians, not only in Sweden.

A similar shift from a pietistic theology, based on personal experiences, toward a more objective, confessional theology also took place in Finland, especially through the new research on Luther. A new ecclesiology, inspired by Gustaf Wingren's dissertation *Luthers lära om kallelsen* (Luther's teaching on vocation), 1942, found its way into the evangelical Lutheran church in Finland, especially within "the young church movement," where the war was seen as a starting point for both a social and a theological awakening. The war also led to closer cooperation between Finnish and Swedish theologians, and some of the leading Finnish theologians studied in Lund.

The new research on Luther's theology, inspired by Lund, led to a shift in Finnish theology toward a stronger emphasis on creation and vocation. At the same time, a more critical attitude toward the traditional pietistic theology could be noticed. In 1952 a book on "the secular and the spiritual" *(Mallinen ja Hengellinen)*, written by Erkki Niinivaara, caused a very lively debate within the church. The book showed how Luther's theology of creation and vocation could motivate the church's responsibility in social ethics. The debate moved beyond church circles and became a public discussion in the newspapers. The book was very critical toward the low-church movement, which was accused of not taking the Lutheran tradition seriously. Niinivaara sharply criticized the concept of *ecclesiola* and the need to draw "frontiers against the world" which characterized the pietistic tradition. This ecclesiology sees the church only as a minority of believers and forgets that the gospel has to be preached to all people, and it tends to look at the spiritual realm as superior to the secular, in direct opposition to Luther's view, Niinivaara claimed. The book was the first one in Finland to present Lundensian theology in a popular way and to evaluate Finnish Lutheranism from the perspective of the new research on Luther in Lund. According to Niinivaara, "the world's most Lutheran country" had very clearly moved away from Luther's original thoughts.

There are similarities between Niinivaara's criticism and Karl Barth's criticism of German Lutheranism after the war, although Niinivaara was not directly motivated by Barth but by Lundensian theology. On the other hand, impulses from Barth came through ecumenical circles, and some theologians used Barth's theology as an argument for closer contact between church and systematic theology.

The new interest in the church led to a shift in theology in Norway as well. Already in the 1930s influences from dialectic theology and the Luther renaissance had reached Norway, even though Barth's theology never got a broad reception in Norwegian theology. At MF, Ole Hallesby's pietistic theology was attacked by younger teachers, especially Leiv Aalen. Hallesby had been influenced by the theology he met in Erlangen, with its strong emphasis on the Christian's spiritual experiences. In Hallesby's theology, Scripture and experience were the central elements. On the other hand, Aalen developed a theology based on Scripture and confession (especially the *Book of Concord*). Aalen was influenced by "new Lutheranism" and developed a strong criticism of Hallesby's pietistic theology, which was accused of subjectivism. Hallesby did not influence theological students as much as people within the lay Christian movement in Norway and other Nordic countries. He was for many decades a leader of the conservative movement in the church, strongly attacking the liberal side. Aalen had a much deeper influence on the students at MF, with his emphasis on the objective elements of Lutheran belief — church, ministry, and sacraments.

In Denmark Regin Prenter became the leading theological thinker after the war. He was inspired by Barth and Nygren and the other young theologians from Lund. Prenter's theology may be seen as a parallel to the theological development in the other Nordic countries, with its emphasis on the church. In 1944 he wrote a very important declaration, *Kirken og Retten i den aktuelle Situation* (The church and the law in the present situation), in which he underlined the church's responsibility for the law, especially as this was threatened by a totalitarian ideology without limits. In it he reformulated the Lutheran view of the two kingdoms or regiments in a way similar to the reformulation that took place in Lund and in Eivind Berggrav's theology during the war. A common "Nordic Lutheranism" became more and more visible.

Also in Denmark, the new interest in the church was combined with a strong criticism of the old pietistic theology. An example is Poul G. Lindhardt's book *Vækkelser og kirkelige retninger* (Awakenings and different directions in church life), which was published in 1949 in connection with the 100th anniversary of the Danish constitution. The book was a polemic against the awakening movements, which Lindhardt said caused severe damage to the church because of their distinction between the "living congregation" and outsiders. Lindhardt wanted to put the parish congregation in the middle of his ecclesiology, without any classification of who were the most believing ones, who belonged to the "inner circle," and who were to be characterized only as "habitual Christians." Lindhardt, who since 1942 had been a professor of theology in Århus, spoke for church democracy, based on the parish.

Hal Koch, a theological professor in Copenhagen, had similar views as Lindhardt on church democracy. In his ecclesiology he was influenced by Grundtvig's view of the empirical church as "an earthly guest room" for the activity of the Holy Spirit. Koch emphasized the freedom of the church and argued for close cooperation between church and culture.

Prenter's ecclesiology, building on the theology of the Reformation, differed considerably from Lindhardt's and Koch's. He focused on the Word and the sacraments as the basic elements of the church, and with his liturgical and sacramental attitude was opposed to a subjective theology that did not stress the objective elements in Christian faith. He also helped create a liturgical renewal in Denmark, which led to an integration of baptism and communion in ordinary services. Prenter and his colleague in Copenhagen, Kristen Ejner Skydsgaard, became the main representatives in Denmark for a new tendency in Danish theology that was characterized as "ecumenical Lutheranism." In Denmark, however, this theology was not supported by the majority of the folk church members.

This new interest in the church during and after the war was a common trait in most Nordic countries. It was weaker in Iceland, where liberal theology still had a strong position, than in the other countries, although a shift of paradigms also became visible there, especially in Sigurbjörn Einarsson's theology, which was influenced by the Uppsala school of exegesis and kerygmatic theology. In his own periodical, *Vidförli*, he published in the years 1947-55 news from European church life and also criticized liberal theologians for being isolated and outdated. When he later became a bishop, he was supported by both liberals and conservatives, and beginning in the 1960s discussions between the two groups of theologians — the liberal and the conservative, pietistically influenced theologians within the Christian lay organizations like the YMCA/YWCA — came to an end.

Reintroduction of Theological Controversies — a Norwegian Debate on Hell

Although there were several common traits in Nordic Lutheranism the first years after the war — especially the new focus on ecclesiology and the criticism of the old liberal and pietistic traditions — new controversies soon became visible. In Iceland the old controversies between liberal and conservative theology were deepened after the war, before the period of tension started in the 1960s. And in other countries there were sharp discussions between different theological groups in the 1950s.

In Norway a discussion about eternal punishment between Hallesby and the bishop of the Hamar diocese, Kristian Schjelderup, made clear that there were still considerable disagreements between different groups and traditions within Norwegian theology. To a certain extent the two theological faculties were seen as representatives of two different models of theology, although there were also internal disagreements in each faculty.

The debate started when Hallesby, in a radio sermon on January 23, 1953, provoked many listeners with his words on eternal damnation: "I suppose that this night I preach to many people who know in their heart that they are not really converted. But you know that if you in this very moment fell down dead, you would fall directly into hell." In many respects Hallesby's words were typical of a traditional pietistic way of preaching. But when a liberal newspaper in Oslo, *Dagbladet*, published a sharp criticism of Hallesby the next day, a long public debate started that involved many participants, both from the church and from society as a whole. Almost all newspapers took part in the debate. Strangely enough, Hallesby himself did not participate in the first part of the debate, but later on he felt it necessary to make it clear why he had talked so directly about eternal punishment.

What pushed him into the debate was an article by Schjelderup one week later in *Aftenposten*, the biggest newspaper in Norway. Although Schjelderup admitted that he hadn't listened to the sermon, he said he reacted very strongly against what he had read about it, and he strongly warned against a way of preaching that used threats of hell as a means of converting people. To do this is not only wrong, he wrote, it is dangerous. "No one of us has the right to judge the fate of our fellow human beings, and even less the right to condemn them to eternal suffering." He also proclaimed that he could not accept the dogma on eternal punishment as a genuine part of the Christian faith. On the contrary, he found such a message directly opposed to the belief in a loving Father. In his answer to this article, Hallesby referred to article 17 in the Augsburg Confession, claiming he was in total accordance with the Lutheran confession and that it was Schjelderup who ought to be criticized for his unbiblical views.

The discussion went on between supporters of the two adversaries, and brought to life again the old controversy between liberal and conservative theology from the first decades of the twentieth century. Hallesby was supported by the pietistic movement within the Inner Mission and other lay organizations. A strong supporter was Carl Fr. Wisløff, who at that time was rector of the Practical Theological Seminary at MF. In a commentary Wisløff wrote that he found it very strange that a bishop could deny a teaching that was clearly established both in the Bible and in the confession. From the conservative side, many claimed that Schjelderup could not be accepted as a bishop as long as he proclaimed his unbiblical view. Pressure against the bishop increased, even among the clergy and within the congregations in his own diocese, and in June Schjelderup saw no other option than to ask the Ministry of

Church Affairs to decide whether his opinions were in accordance with the Lutheran confession.

This meant that the discussion could no longer be seen only as a theological controversy within the church. Now it had become a question of tolerance and limits within the folk church. First, a decision had to be made whether the government and the ministry could take a stand in a theological issue. Then all the bishops and the two theological faculties were asked to give their statements. All bishops agreed that the Church of Norway was a confessing church, but they differed regarding Schjelderup's future within the church. Two of the eight bishops said his view was in conflict with the Lutheran confession, and one of them said he ought to resign. The same conclusion was drawn by the professors at MF, where Hallesby and Wisløff belonged, while on the other hand the university faculty concluded that Schjelderup should continue as a bishop. If he withdrew, many people would see themselves as homeless within the folk church, they claimed. In February 1954 the ministry concluded that the bishop had not put himself outside the confession.

The Swedish Debate on Academic Theology

The relationship between the Church of Sweden and the theological faculties gradually changed after the war, and the differences between academic theology and church theology became more and more obvious. In this the Swedish situation differed from the Norwegian one. In the Schjelderup case the close link between the church and the theological faculties had been underlined.

In Sweden, however, the attitude toward theology and religion was strongly influenced by a professor in practical philosophy in Uppsala, Ingemar Hedenius, who in 1949 published the book *Tro och vetande* (Faith and knowledge). This book was the starting point for a debate on academic theology, and the most radical participants in the debate claimed that the theological faculties no longer should be part of the universities, because of their "unscientific" methods.

In Uppsala Hedenius's criticism was met by attempts at dialogue and accommodation to his scientific ideals. The theologians there were influenced by Anglo-Saxon philosophical schools that underlined the distinction between faith and science. A leading theologian in Uppsala, Axel Gyllenkrok, took the first steps toward a new understanding of theology that brought it close to the history of ideas and religious science. Although some of the leading professors in Lund, like Wingren, Nygren, and Aulén, defended the scientific character of theology and criticized Hedenius's ideological basis, the development in both faculties more and more went in the same direction. In the beginning of the seventies, all formal links between the Church of Sweden and the theological faculties were broken, and the theological disciplines were changed. Systematic theology became "science of faith and worldviews," and practical theology was developed into "science of church and societies." In both Uppsala and Lund, the empirical and scientific character of theology was underlined.

Although the formal bonds between theology and church were broken, in reality there were links. Most of the theological teachers were ordained clergy who still influenced the theological thinking within the Church of Sweden. This has gradually changed, especially during the last twenty years, in which a growing number of teachers belong to other churches or to no Christian church at all. The Church of Sweden therefore has established its own pastoral institutes in Lund and Uppsala (1980), and in 1990 the research council of the church (Svenska kyrkans Forskningsråd) was established in Uppsala.

The Relation between Theology and Church in the Other Nordic Countries

The development of academic theology in Sweden differs from that of the other Nordic countries. In the Finnish academic world there was less conflict between theology and science partly because of the national agreement between different scientific disciplines. However, it became increasingly clear that the relationship between church and theology had also grown looser than before. One of the leading professors in theology,

Osmo Tiililä, underlined the unique and autonomous character of theology. The influence from Karl Barth became visible when Tiililä presented the Finnish theology to the General Assembly of the Lutheran World Federation (LWF) in Helsinki in 1963, in *Finnish Theology Past and Present*.

Tiililä himself became more and more critical of the Evangelical Lutheran Church in Finland. In 1961 he withdrew from his ministry, and after the General Assembly in 1963 he left the church. This led to a discussion whether a nonmember of the church could still be a professor in systematic theology. Tiililä was allowed to continue as professor, but when he resigned in 1967 a debate on the task of theology started, especially when Arne Siirala was appointed as his successor. Siirala was influenced by the Swedish professor Ragnar Bring, and there were strong reactions against him, especially from circles within the awakening movement. Siirala was accused of being too radical to take part in the education of the clergy. As a result of the discussions, Siirala decided not to accept the position, and instead Seppo A. Teinonen became the new professor in systematic theology.

Denmark offers no parallel to the Swedish debate on the scientific character of theology. There the close cooperation between the folk church and the theological institutions was stressed, and theologians like Knud E. Løgstrup formulated a view of theology that could be accepted both in church and society. Løgstrup's theology of creation, based on the idea of the universal character of Christianity, gave opportunities to interpret modern culture in a Christian perspective. Løgstrup was respected also by nontheologians, and he strongly contributed to the positive evaluation of theology in Denmark.

In the sixties, however, Danish theology also was characterized by a growing antagonism between different theological schools. The leadership in the folk church after the war was held by people who were deeply influenced by the new folk church theology, based on Grundtvig's ideas. As a reaction, new initiatives were taken which showed a growing polarization within the church. In 1964 theologians who belonged to the Inner Mission and the high-church movement presented a declaration called *Kirkens Ja og Nej* (The church's yes and no). Regin Prenter and one of the bishops also signed this declaration, which protested the tendencies in Danish theology and church life to underestimate the Bible and the confession. The best example of this tendency was, according to the declaration, the ordination of female clergy, which was seen as a serious attack on the church's old tradition. In his book *Kirkens embede* (The ministry of the church), Prenter further developed his arguments against female clergy, and he also published a popular dogmatic book, *Kirkens tro* (The faith of the church), with a clear conservative profile.

Another sign of the growing controversies in Danish theology was the establishing of Menighedsfakultetet in Århus, an independent theological institution inspired by the Norwegian MF. Although the institution has not yet gained official status, it has influenced a growing number of Danish clergy and given them a conservative theological education. In Copenhagen, a similar initiative was taken to establish a conservative theological school, Dansk Bibel-Institut (The Danish Bible Institute).

In Norway there were some parallels to the Danish controversies. The old antagonism between liberals and conservatives, institutionalized in the tension between the two theological faculties, was upheld in the discussion on female clergy. Access to the ministry had in principle been open for women since 1938, but no women had been ordained before Ingrid Bjerkås, a nearly sixty-year-old woman, was ordained by Kristian Schjelderup in Hamar March 19, 1961. This event was welcomed in liberal circles within the church and in feminist organizations, but led to strong reactions from the conservative part of the church. Six of the nine bishops said ordination of female pastors was in clear contradiction to Scripture and confession, and they said they would refuse to cooperate with female clergy. They also suggested that both clergy and laypeople should boycott Bjerkås. The six bishops were supported by most of the lay Christian organizations in Norway and by the conservative part of the clergy, especially those who had studied at MF.

For many years the number of female clergy in Norway was very small, but after 1980 the numbers started to grow. In 1995, 11 percent of the clergy in active service were women, and in the last years the percentage of ordained female candidates has been over 40 percent. Another event was the appointment of the first female bishop, Rosemarie

Köhn, in the Hamar diocese. She was appointed by the Labour government, but in the church vote she came second, beaten by only one male. Today two of the eleven Norwegian bishops are women, and one of them has received her education from MF and was the first ordained woman to become a teacher at the faculty. The issue of female clergy clearly is no longer a matter of discussion within the Church of Norway, even though there are still clergymen who refuse to cooperate with female clergy.

Systematic theology was a major discipline at MF after the war, represented first by the strict confessional theology of Leiv Aalen, but in later years by more moderate conservative Lutherans like Ivar Asheim and Torleiv Austad, who have both been active in the ecumenical movement. Systematic theology played a less important role at TF in the first decades after the war. The church historian Einar Molland was a leading professor after the war, together with Nils A. Dahl, who had written a very important dissertation entitled *Das Volk Gottes* in 1941. As a professor in New Testament exegesis, later at Yale University, he had a special interest in ecclesiology and in the discussion on the "historical Jesus." The interest in systematic theology grew in the 1970s, especially after Inge Lønning's dissertation *Kanon im Kanon* (1971), a discussion on the problem of norms in theology.

The links between church and theology are still close in Norway. Not only do the theological professors vote for new bishops, but church legislation still demands that they belong to the Church of Norway. But the law allows for exceptions, and today all three theological faculties, TF, MF, and MHS (the Missionary High School in Stavanger), have in principle opened up for non-Lutheran teachers, but at the same time they all underline their close link to the Church of Norway.

New Ecumenical and International Impulses in Nordic Theology

The new international and ecumenical organizations established after the war, especially the World Council of Churches (WCC) and the LWF, not only gave the Nordic folk churches an opportunity to come into closer contact and cooperation with churches from other parts of the world, they also permitted access to new models of theological thinking that in turn gave new impulses to traditional Lutheran theology.

An eminent example of how Nordic theology was influenced by the new ecumenism is Seppo A. Teinonen's development, especially after he was asked by the LWF to be an official observer at the Second Vatican Council. In his writings during and after the council, the ecumenical character of his theology becomes more and more obvious. Teinonen's role during the council led to much closer contact between the Lutheran and the Catholic churches in Finland. As early as 1968 the Roman Catholic Church was accepted as a full member of the Finnish Ecumenical Council. For many years Teinonen was involved in ecumenical discussions with the Catholic Church, and his ecumenical theology contributed a lot to theological study of the ministry of the church. However, he withdrew from the study committee in the early seventies because he refused to accept female clergy. As a theological teacher he still had great influence, introducing Roman Catholic theology to Finnish theological students. Teinonen himself did not convert to the Roman Catholic Church until he had ended his academic career.

Vatican II also influenced Swedish theology and led to a growing interest in Roman Catholic theology there, especially in intellectual circles. In Norway, Einar Molland was influenced by the council, and he acted as chairman for the joint Lutheran–Roman Catholic study commission (1967-71). In Finland the contact with Orthodox theology has also been influential within the Lutheran church.

Important ecumenical influences also came from international organizations like the WCC, and the General Assembly in Uppsala in 1968 introduced a lot of new models of theological and ecumenical thinking to both Sweden and the other Nordic countries. In the late 1960s and 1970s influences from political theology and the theology of liberation became visible even in Nordic theology.

At the same time, there was a growing skepticism toward ecumenical impulses emanating from the WCC, especially in Finland and Norway. The conservative side issued warnings against the growing liberalism and radicalism within the ecumenical movement. The criticism in Denmark was less visible, but then again, Danish theology was less open to the new ecumenical impulses in the first decades after the war. However, the interest for European ecumenical cooperation grew stronger in Denmark, and Danish theologians and church leaders played an important role in the formation of the Conference of European Churches.

In Norway some of the leading young theologians started discussions on social ethics from a more radical perspective than before, and traditional theological thinking was criticized for being too "bourgeois." A forerunner in Norway for a modern social ethical theology was Tor Aukrust. In 1967-68 he published two volumes of his book *Mennesket i samfunnet* (Man in society), where he challenged traditional models within theological ethics, claiming that the church needed to analyze the changes that had happened within modern society. Aukrust combined his interest in an undogmatic socialism with an undogmatic theology, and his books challenged young theologians in Norway who were unsatisfied with traditional theology. In the following years, a slogan among some of these theologians was "theologically conservative, politically radical." Many of the new politically radical theologians, sympathizing with the socialists, came from pietistic backgrounds, and most had studied at MF or at the missionary school in Stavanger, and they wanted to underline the continuity with their theological heritage while at the same time criticizing the political implications of the traditional way of thinking in church theology.

Gradually, impulses from Third World theology also led to a shift of theological models among the young radical theologians in Norway. Influences from Latin American theology of liberation and from South African black theology found their way into Norwegian theology, and there was a growing awareness of the contextual character of all theology.

The influences from modern ecumenical theology and liberation theology are also obvious in the other Nordic countries. The Faith and Order document *Baptism, Eucharist and Ministry* (1982) has been thoroughly discussed in all churches and has been an important source of theological inspiration during the last two decades. The discussions with the Roman Catholic Church, leading to the *Joint Declaration on Justification* (1997), have also had great impact on theological work in the Nordic countries.

The Porvoo Agreement (ratified 1994/95, signed 1996) is important to Nordic church life, although Denmark has chosen not to sign this agreement with the Anglican Church. Impulses from Anglicanism had influenced Nordic theology after the war, and in Sweden the contact with Anglican theology had already been strong before the war. Discussions between the Anglican Church and some of the Nordic churches around 1950 led to no substantial changes. Bishop Berggrav of Oslo concluded that the Church of Norway could not accept any agreement with the Anglicans that implied any doubt on the apostolicity of the Norwegian church. This conclusion did not ignore the conversations' documentation of how much the Anglican and Lutheran churches had in common theologically and historically.

In 1989 the official representatives of four Anglican churches and eight Nordic and Baltic churches began theological conversations again. The Porvoo Common Statement included the text of the Porvoo Declaration, which the participants commended for acceptance to their churches. The report is named after the Porvoo (Borgå) Cathedral in Finland, where the Eucharist was celebrated on the final Sunday of the conversations. The purpose of the agreement was to draw the churches into a new and closer relationship for the sake of greater unity and more effective mission. The Porvoo Agreement means that for the first time the Anglican churches in Britain and Ireland have moved into visible communion with other national churches in Europe.

Critics have asked whether the agreement strengthens the bishop's ministry too much, changing the focus from the basic ministry of the pastors and reducing the influence of the synod. A main issue in the discussions has been the question of the historic episcopate. The Baltic churches have not always had bishops, but now not only are there bishops in their churches, but bishops who stand in the historic succession of the laying on of hands. The churches of Sweden and Finland, like the Anglican churches, have inherited the historic succession. In Denmark, Norway, and Iceland the churches have preserved the continuity in the episcopal office, but at the time of the Reformation they did so by an occasional priestly or presbyterial ordination.

The Porvoo Common Statement argues that "the mutual acknowledgment of churches and ministries is theologically prior to the use of the sign," and its resumption "does not imply an adverse judgment on the ministries of those churches" that previously did not use it. In a statement, the Church of Norway's General Synod underlined that the apostolicity of the church is manifested in the church when the church is faithful to the apostolic faith and the apostolic calling. It is manifested in the intention to be apostolic in faith and life, sent by Christ to the world. If the Anglican churches can accept the comprehensive understanding of the apostolicity of the church and apostolic succession in the Porvoo report, then there is a basis for church fellowship, according to the Church of Norway. The church accepts that the historical episcopal succession is an important sign, but not a condition, for the manifestation of church fellowship.

The Porvoo Agreement has led to a situation where churches like the Church of Norway normally invite bishops from churches that have maintained the historical episcopate to the consecrations of bishops — together with representatives from other churches. The agreement has also opened a door to a full sacramental fellowship with Anglican churches.

Debates on Ethical Issues

The discussions on female clergy led for some decades to serious controversies in Nordic theology. Lately ethical issues like homosexuality have caused more discussion, and in all Nordic countries theologians have been involved in this. In Norway the bishops' meeting divided on the issue in 1995, on the background of a report written by a commission on which all three theological faculties and homosexuals and lesbians were represented. The disagreement between the bishops led to a public debate, and the old divisions between liberals and conservatives were again used to characterize the different opinions within the church. Today the discussions are conducted in a quieter tone, and the whole issue has been referred to the dogmatic committee of the church (Den norske kirkes lærenemnd). In this debate, not only will the issue of homosexuality be discussed, but the whole theological framework for the issue, including questions on the authority and use of the Bible in theology and ethics.

In the other Nordic countries there have been similar processes, including theological commissions presenting reports on homosexuality and the church. The general tendency has been toward a more liberal view on this issue in all the Nordic countries, although there are still groups that claim that acceptance of homosexual practice is contrary to the Word of God.

Other ethical issues discussed in the Nordic countries today usually don't lead to theological controversies. There is considerable agreement in matters like bioethics, environmental ethics, and global justice, and at least disagreements in issues like these are not due to theological differences.

Tendencies in Recent Theological Education and Research

Recently Nordic theological education has undergone important changes. Traditionally only a few theological faculties offered such education. In some countries, especially Sweden, a lot of institutions now offer theological studies. This is of course a challenge to the traditional institutions, especially the faculties in Lund and Uppsala, who have to adjust to the prospect of increased competition. In Finland and Denmark the situation is not so complicated, because theological education is still dominated by the traditional theological faculties in Åbo and Helsinki (Finland) and Copenhagen and Århus (Denmark).

A tendency toward more competition among theological institutions also prevails in Norway. However, the three theological faculties, TF, MF, and MHS, are still the only ones allowed to give a complete theological education for the clergy. There has been a paradigm shift in theological education the last years, with much more emphasis on an integrated study where practical and theoretical theology meet in a fruitful way. Of course, influences from liberation theology and contextual models of theology have led to this new way of thinking, and often this model is characterized as a "practice-theory-practice" model.

In all Nordic countries the effects of internationalization and globalization have challenged the theological institutions in new ways. For the time being, the implementation of the "Bologna process" has high priority. The tendency toward more compatibility within the education system will improve the situation for students who want to study abroad or for foreign students who want to take exams at a Nordic theological faculty.

Obviously, theological research has become a more important matter than ever in all the Nordic countries. In an environment of increased competition for funding among different academic disciplines, the theological institutions have given good research projects high priority, trying to establish excellent groups of researchers who work together. The traditional individualistic way of doing research is being more and more replaced by common projects, and even projects where theologians work with scientists from other disciplines, like social sciences, history, medicine, technology, etc.

Traditional Revivalism after the War

Developments in postwar theology in the Nordic countries have often but not always been followed by similar developments in spirituality. On the other hand, new models of spirituality have also influenced theological thinking and opened it to new issues.

All Nordic countries the first years after the war were characterized, as we have seen, by theological criticism against the traditional spirituality within the low-church pietistic movements. In Norway the close co-operation between bishops and leaders of the awakening movements during the war offered hope that the traditional revivalism would still hold a strong position after the war, and many spoke of a "national awakening" to come. But this did not happen, either in Norway or in any other Nordic country.

This revivalism was rooted in the awakening movements in the nineteenth century, many of them with a pietistic background. The influence in Norway from Hans Nielsen Hauge was still vivid, and influences from Swedish awakenings, especially within the "new evangelism," had been visible in parts of the low-church movement. In Sweden, the free church awakening movements were strong, both within the Mission Covenant Church of Sweden and the evangelical movement within the Swedish church (Evangeliska Fosterlands-Stiftelsen [EFS]). The Pentecostal movement had become strong, especially in Sweden and Norway, while in Finland the awakening had found its way into the folk church. In Denmark the traditional awakening movement was mainly to be found within the Inner Mission, with 300,000 members in the 1920s. Traditional awakenings had a shorter history in Iceland, although impulses from the YMCA/YWCA and from Norwegian and Danish Inner Mission reached the island in the first part of the twentieth century.

Already before the war leaders of the traditional awakening movements had seen signs that time was running out for the awakenings, and although there were still reports after the war of local awakenings, these events grew increasingly scattered. The lack of awakenings could — at least for some time — be compensated by another way of recruiting members to the movements. Instead of a sudden conversion, members were increasingly recruited through socialization processes within the movement. This could be achieved by intensified work among children and youth. The expansion of such activities was considerable after the war, and many young persons met the traditional awakening movement through summer camps, where the ideological presuppositions for the awakening still were presented.

This also meant that the social dimension of the movements gradually changed. The work had to concentrate on more than preaching the Word, and it was necessary to include more social and cultural activities to create a climate for socialization. This process has led to new conflicts within the traditional awakening movements, where traditionalists fear that the Christian message will suffer when new methods are used to attract modern people. There have been discussions on the use of music, drama, and dance within many of the traditional awakening movements, and the degree of accommodation to modern cultural expressions has varied a lot. In some movements, as in Laestadianism, the skepticism toward elements from the modern culture has been strong, while other movements, like the YMCA/YWCA and the Inner Mission and similar organizations (like EFS in Sweden), have accommodated modernity much more. This has led to an increase in activities also in many traditional awakening movements, although signs from the last decades indicate that the recruiting process has slowed down. Today the traditional awakening movements face important changes, both structurally and socially, which have to be challenged. There is a tendency toward more bureaucracy and more emphasis on professional work, while the traditional activities, partly based on voluntarism, have slowed down.

The changes within the movements have come not only because of processes within the movements themselves, but are connected also to more general developments in the society. A major factor is the growing urbanization that took place in the Nordic countries after the war. As the traditional awakenings were deeply rooted in rural districts, this led to a weakening of the movements, and the strategies to strengthen their position in urban areas have not always been successful. The cultural changes in the process of urbanization have also created new problems, since the traditional revivalism to a large extent could suppose a common cultural heritage that is no longer present in migrant areas.

Changes in the situation of women have also affected traditional awakenings. Most women today work outside the home, and less time is left for voluntary work within Christian organizations. The general process of secularization and pluralization has also weakened the possibilities for traditional awakenings. Today most people are less informed about the Bible than before, and it is more difficult to argue from a common basis of Christian knowledge. The gap between the awakening movements and society as a whole has increased, and the possibilities for contact with people outside the movements have decreased. Another problem has been the fragmentation caused by the many different organizations within the lay Christian movement. In recent years there have been signs of fusion, as in Norway, where the Inner Mission and a missionary organization (Santalmisjonen) have created a new group called Normisjon.

New Church Activities

The changes within the traditional awakenings are also connected to new developments within the folk churches. After the war, activity within the official church structures increased, especially in urban areas. An important factor here was the building of new churches in the new living areas, churches that were equipped to serve the new church activities. In these churches a new model of spirituality, different from the pietistic spirituality in the awakening movements, became more visible. On the one hand, many Christians from the awakening movement became actively involved in the new church activities and influenced the local congregational boards, but on the other hand the new church activity created a kind of competitiveness between two different kinds of spirituality. In Norway this has led to a withdrawal from the official church structures by some of the main low-church organizations (for example, Norsk Luthersk Misjonssamband).

In Finland there have been controversies between the new pietistic movement and the new folk church movement. A crucial moment in these controversies was Osmo Tiililä's reaction in the early 1960s against the folk church movement, which was accused of preaching a social gospel instead of the old biblical message. The new pietistic movement in Finland reacted against the increased focus on social and diaconal issues within the folk church, and underlined such traditional low-church attitudes as personal conversion and a clear line between true believers and nonbelievers. On the other hand, the new folk church movement criticized the tendency within pietism to create an *ecclesiola in ecclesia*, leading to sharp distinctions within the congregations. The pietistic movement also was accused of clinging too much to traditions and old structures.

The experiences during the war had inspired parts of the Finnish clergy to strengthen the church's national and social responsibility, and the new challenges led to a criticism of the old evangelical movements, which were accused of not being able to understand the present situation, fighting for lost causes. The folk church movement had led to impressive changes in church activities after the war, including work among youth, family counseling, hospital work, and other diaconal activities. Within the structure of the folk church, new models of activities were developed which led to an increase of professionalism and to further differentiations. The developments within diaconal education increased the competence both within the church and in the public social institutions.

The other Nordic countries had similar experiences as Finland, as the new church activities including social and diaconal work created a spirituality that differed from the old pietistic spirituality that concentrated solely on "the one thing needful," the preaching of the gospel to save souls. A more practical spirituality was developed, less dogmatic and less focused on personal spiritual experiences. For modern people in urban areas, this new church activity offered a more attractive way of expressing religious attitudes than the old awakenings.

One of the factors behind the new spirituality was the Oxford movement, which influenced most Nordic countries from the early 1930s and presented an alternative to the pietistic awakenings for modern, intellectual people. In Norway, some of the leading persons behind the new church activity after the war had their background in the Oxford movement.

In Denmark the spirituality within the Grundtvig movement is still present, with its emphasis on the strong link between Christian life and the ordinary human life. The Grundtvig movement is much more differentiated and less structured than the Inner Mission movement, with "freedom" as a slogan. After the war the movement had to face realities; one could no longer speak about an "awakening," and the different factions within Grundtvigianism went in different directions. But still, this movement has had a great influence on Danish church life and culture, and it is still considered a strong alternative both to conservative high-church movements, fundamentalism, and to the more liberal, ecumenical groups within the Danish church.

Liturgy and High-Church Movements

In Sweden and in other Nordic countries a liturgical spirituality was developed within the high-church movement, especially after the war. The leading figure behind the high-church revival was the Swedish pastor Gunnar Rosendal, who was influenced by the Anglo-Catholic tradition with its emphasis on *tidebønn*, renewal of worship and liturgy, the Eucharist, processions, hymns, and a high evaluation of ministry. Rosendal's 1935 book on church renewal, together with the new emphasis on ecclesiology within Swedish theology during and after the war, formed the basis for the high-church program. Like his colleague Bo Giertz, he developed a new type of theology for the church from his base as a parish pastor. They were serving as active parish pastors when doing theology and presenting a renewed ecclesiological program for the church. This movement especially found its way to Lund and Uppsala, where young students were attracted by the liturgical renewal. The traditional revival movements had found support mainly in lower social groups, while the high-church movement became popular among intellectuals and other members of the high society.

The Second Vatican Council led to a breakthrough for high-church movements. The anti-Catholic sentiments in the population were weakened, and a deepened interest in rituals and mysticism recruited new members to the high-church groups. The opening of the ministry for female clergy was, however, a severe problem for the movement, and the gap between high church and folk church has become deeper in recent years, resulting in withdrawal from the folk churches and conversions to the Roman Catholic Church and other churches in the Anglo-Catholic tradition, especially in Sweden and Norway.

New Spiritual Movements within and outside the Folk Churches

The Nordic folk churches have also been challenged by new spiritual movements and awakenings whose roots emanate outside the Nordic churches. Many of these have been imported from the United States, directly or indirectly, and they have had influence within both free churches and folk churches.

The Pentecostal movement became the most powerful of these movements during the twentieth century, promoted by powerful leaders such as Lewi Pethrus in Sweden and Thomas Barratt in Norway. From its beginning in Los Angeles in 1907, the Pentecostal movement combined elements from American revivalism, and its Anglo-American character is obvious. Most of the members of Pentecostal congregations, especially in the first decades, emanated from the lower classes, and the movement has been skeptical toward traditional theological education.

After the war, America also influenced Nordic church life through new ecumenical awakening campaigns. The Baptist pastor Billy Graham was the most outstanding example of this. In 1954 he was invited to Sweden by the Swedish Baptist Church, and a great awakening campaign was held in Stockholm before 50,000 persons. The campaign was ecumenical in orientation, and even the bishop of Stockholm, Manfred Björkquist, took part in it. Similar campaigns were held in other Nordic countries. In Norway Graham preached in the main sports arena in Oslo, Ullevål Stadium. Such campaigns inspired local ecumenical campaigns, and in Norway Graham inspired a Norwegian lay preacher, John Olav Larssen, who drew thousands to another stadium in Oslo in 1957.

In the late 1960s the charismatic movement with its Anglo-American roots challenged the established folk churches and revival movements in the Nordic countries. In Norway the low-church movements were divided in their views; some refused to accept the charismatic movement, while others tried to integrate some of the main impulses into the traditional spirituality. This openness led to the establishment of the "OASE" movement within the Lutheran church. This movement brings together people from various charismatic traditions.

In the last decades, new movements with charismatic backgrounds have influenced the traditional spirituality in the Nordic countries. In the early 1970s the Jesus movement inspired young people with its unorthodox way of preaching and living, and later on movements like the

Vineyard have brought new impulses to the Nordic countries from the Anglo-American world. The establishment of "Christian centers" and movements like "Livets ord" (The Word of Life) in Uppsala also has to be seen as a result of the charismatic influences, especially from the United States. The impulses from Kenneth Hagin and other representatives of a "strong" charismatic theology inspired Ulf Ekman in Uppsala and other founders of neo-Pentecostal congregations in the Nordic countries.

A New Religious Spirituality

Up until the 1970s, religious sociologists predicted the decline and fall of religion and spirituality. The secularization process was seen as an inevitable movement toward a society where the religious dimension became more and more marginalized. This prophecy has not been confirmed. On the contrary, the last decades have revealed a new interest in religion and a new spirituality that has been described as a "resacralization" and a "retraditionalization" that has changed the whole process of secularization and led to a more nuanced evaluation of the role of religion and spirituality, even in the secular Western societies.

A part of this new religious movement has had little or no contact with traditional Christian spirituality. The New Age movement has its main roots in Eastern religious thought, especially Hinduism and Buddhism, and it is possible to detect similarities between old gnostic philosophy and modern religious ideas of a divine, cosmic energy. Still, the challenges — both from other traditional religions because of immigration to the Nordic countries and from New Age — have inspired groups within the churches to open up dialogues on religion and spirituality. The Nordic missionary movement Areopagos has played an important part in these dialogues.

The new interest in religion has also influenced church life more directly. The mystical traditions have been revitalized, and interest in medieval church life has been increasing, also outside the high-church movement. Religiously motivated rituals like the use of candles both in the church and at specific events have also become more common. In

Norway religious sociologists have analyzed the phenomenon that took place before the Royal Castle in January 1991, in the days after the death of King Olav V, where thousands of people lit candles. A renewed interest in pilgrimages has also influenced Nordic church life.

Thus are the Nordic folk churches challenged to integrate the new spirituality in a way that strengthens them and offers new opportunities to communicate the Christian faith in our time. Theology is challenged to help interpret the religious feelings of ordinary people and bring them into contact with the traditions of Christian faith.

9 Nordic Heroes of Church and State

Many persons played key roles in Nordic history since World War II. In this chapter we examine some theological and political figures, and some who bridge the gap between religion and politics, in brief biographical sketches.

The following sketches present one theologian and one politician from each of the four countries discussed in earlier chapters. The profiles of Danes Jens Nørregaard and Bodil Koch are written by Peter Lodberg, those of Finns Martti Simojoki and Urho Kekkonen are by Aila Lauha, those of Norwegians Eivind Berggrav and Gro Harlem Brundtland are by Gunnar Heiene, and those of Swedes Anders Nygren and Olof Palme are by Björn Ryman.

Jens Nørregaard: An Ecumenical Pioneer in Denmark

Jens Skouboe Nørregaard was professor of church history at the University of Copenhagen from 1923 until his death in 1953. He was born in 1887 and graduated in theology in 1910. From 1911 to 1914 he studied theology in Germany, Switzerland, Italy, England, and Scotland. During his studies in Berlin he was inspired by Adolf von Harnack's seminars on Saint Augustine's *Confessions*. In 1928 he did his doctoral thesis on Augustine. All through his life and work he took inspiration from Harnack and liberal theology. In most of his publications he looks upon church history as carried forward by individuals with a special religious and theological personality.

From 1942 to 1948 Nørregaard served as the rector of the University of Copenhagen, and because of his very fine administrative skills he took a leading role in Danish church life. Among other positions, he was a member of the Faith and Order Movement Continuation Committee and the board of the Nordic Ecumenical Institute in Sigtuna, Sweden. He took part in most of the important ecumenical conferences in preparation for the establishment of the WCC, and was a member of the Danish delegation to the First Assembly of the WCC in Amsterdam in 1948. In 1939, together with the bishop of Copenhagen, H. Fuglsang-Damgaard, he took the initiative to establish the Ecumenical Council in Denmark, and he served as its chairman from 1941 to 1942.

From 1933 on he involved himself deeply in the German church struggle. Through the ecumenical movement he established a very broad network of contacts with congregations and pastors in the Confessing Church of Germany and followed intensely the discussion and practice of the Aryan Paragraph in the German churches and the persecution of German Jews. Just after 1933, when German Jews left Germany because of persecution and anti-Semitism, a number of committees were established in Denmark to help Jewish refugees. The archbishop of Canterbury encouraged especially the Danish churches to take a leading role, and in 1938 Nørregaard and others formed a committee called the Relief Committee for Non-Aryan Christians. He considered this work an integral part of his Christian commitment and the responsibility of the Evangelical Lutheran Church of Denmark. After the Second World War, in 1945 Nørregaard was active in establishing a new committee that would serve the more than 200,000 German refugees awaiting return to their homes in Germany. He was convinced that reconciliation with Germany and the reorganization of the German churches were very important to the establishment of peace and prosperity in Europe.

Jens Nørregaard was awarded doctor of honor degrees in Uppsala in 1932, in Oslo in 1945, and at Saint Andrews, Scotland, in 1951.

PETER LODBERG

Bodil Koch: The Architect of the Modern Welfare Church

One of the most influential politicians in the development of the Evangelical Lutheran Church of Denmark after World War II was Bodil Koch. She lived from 1903 to 1972 and was known as an outspoken participant in the public debate about the relationship between church, state, and society.

Already in 1943 Koch showed her strong commitment to issues of justice and democracy when on behalf of Danish women she protested to the German representative in Denmark during the German occupation, Dr. Werner Best, against the persecution of Danish Jews. The same year she took the initiative in forming one of the first grassroots movements in Denmark, called Folkevirke (People's Action), formally established in 1944. The aim was to encourage and educate Danish women to participate in public life and political democracy.

Folkevirke became the popular basis for her political involvement. In 1947 she was elected to Parliament (Folketinget) as representative of the Social Democratic Party (the Labour Party) in Herning, a small town at that time in the middle of Jutland. She represented her constituency for more than twenty years, and through the years built a very close relationship with her electorate. Her motto was: In all your work think of Herning, which in Danish makes a proverb: "I al din gerning, tænk på Herning."

In 1950 she became the first female minister of church affairs in the history of Denmark, and the world. Her tenure lasted only a couple months, because the government had to resign and leave the power to the Liberal Party. In 1953 she was elected to the same position again, and served for more than thirteen years under different prime ministers: Hans Hedtoft, H. C. Hansen, Viggo Kampmann, and Jens Otto Krag. She became minister of culture in 1966 and resigned in 1968, when the Social Democrats lost power.

Koch took an active part in politics and served as a minister during the time Denmark developed from a farmer society to a modern industrialized society. The political, economical, and social program of the Social Democratic Party was to establish a modern welfare society in which the state secures the basic social services and education for all. The economic instrument to establish a more just and fair society is the tax system, which gradually levels the economic differences among the citizens toward more equality.

It is a credit to Koch's long-lasting achievements that she succeeded in organizing the Evangelical Lutheran Church as part of the social welfare society. According to Koch, the church should also understand itself as a church for all, i.e., for the whole Danish population. She wanted the church to be comprehensive and spacious *(rummelig)*, and to include people with strong and weak feelings of identity with it. At the same time, she encouraged it to be a lively church with serious and strong theological debates among the different theological schools and movements. Her central theme was what she called *ny folkekirkelighed*, i.e., a renewed feeling of solidarity with the Lutheran church, which serves the whole people. This was also a sociological fact during her time as minister of church affairs, when approximately 95 percent of the Danish population belonged to the Lutheran church. In her efforts to open the church to the people and to encourage them to understand the Lutheran church as their own, Koch was very clear about the theological identity of the Lutheran Church of Denmark. Her understanding of Christianity was based on a Lutheran anthropology of freedom and a Lutheran ecclesiology based on Word and sacraments. As a theologian educated at the University of Copenhagen, she held the pastoral office in the church as very important and was a strong supporter of the ordination of women, which was established in 1948 but was still not recognized by all congregations at that time.

In 1964 she took the initiative in establishing a new commission to propose a future structure of the Lutheran church (Strukturkommissionen). The church also had to adjust to the rapid developments of society, and the commission came up with a number of recommendations about the future structure. A new structure for ecumenical work was proposed together with the establishment of special ministries for university students and special positions in Christian education. The results of the commission were challenged by a number of influential conservative bishops, laypeople, and civil servants in the Ministry of Church Affairs. For several years nothing happened with the recommendations, but it is interesting that today most of them have been implemented in some measure — not as one big program but as small changes along the way.

Bodil Koch's lasting achievement was twofold. She changed the policy of the Social Democratic Party to make it one of the strongest supporters of the Lutheran church as the church of the people. At the same time, she adjusted the Lutheran church to the new welfare society in the framework of the existing relationship between state and church as formulated in the Danish Constitution from 1849 and renewed in 1953. She had a clear vision of the future of the Lutheran church and its role in Danish society, but at the same time a well-tuned feeling of what it takes in daily church politics and administration to sail a ship like the Lutheran Church of Denmark. The future will tell if she only helped prolong the days of the Lutheran church as the national church of the people or if her vision and efforts had a long-lasting effect on both the Danish people and its church.

PETER LODBERG

Martti Simojoki

Martti Simojoki, who served as bishop and archbishop in Finland during the postwar period, altogether for almost thirty years, was one of the most influential Finnish figures in the twentieth century. Simojoki, whose name originally was Simelius, was a pastor's son. His home was shaped by pietistic religiosity of the revival movement, "the Awakened" of Ostrobothnia. A further heritage of his home was warm patriotism.

During his student years Simojoki participated in student activities, becoming a member of the nationalistic Academic Karelia Society. He was also eager to promote the position of the Finnish language in the university and in Finnish society, and as an expression of that view he changed his own surname to a more Finnish-sounding Simojoki.

After his ordination he worked in Christian associations, as a teacher and as a parish pastor. He also started work on his dissertation at the University of Helsinki, and received his doctorate in practical theology in 1948. His dissertation, "Preaching and Teaching," focused on the pedagogical functions of sermons. He wrote several other books as well, mainly of a meditative and devotional nature.

During the Finnish-Soviet wars Simojoki served as a military chaplain. The war profoundly transformed his religious and social thinking. He became a member of the association Asevelipapit (Priests for Brothers in Arms), which was founded by young pastors who were from different religious groups in the church but had a common vision: to develop pastoral care among Finnish men both in war and peace.

After the war this activity expanded, and much of the new postwar social program of the Lutheran church was built on the basis of it. The new theological periodical Vartija (The Watchman) was founded to promote these views, and Simojoki was the publication's first editor in chief. He also was active in a reform movement called "Neo-folk-church-movement," which endeavored to promote ecclesiastical reforms such as pastoral care in hospitals and family counseling, and had as its center the new laymen's training institute in Järvenpää. Simojoki was the director of this institute from 1950 to 1951.

Between 1951 and 1958 Simojoki served as the bishop of Mikkeli, until he became the first bishop of the newly established diocese of Helsinki (1959-64). In the early 1960s significant policy disputes took place within the church. The so-called neo-pietistic groups in particular challenged the church leaders by claiming that the church had followed a course that was too social ethical and even secularized.

Simojoki had a good understanding of religious pietistic views, but he wanted at the same time to stress the church's social responsibility and the necessity of cultural dialogue. His tranquil and fatherly style of speaking became well-known to the whole nation.

In 1964 Simojoki became the archbishop of Finland. He had thus to face the most critical years of radicalism, which often was directed toward church and religion. The greatest public attention was aroused in 1964 when he openly condemned the way a Finnish writer, Hannu Salama, dealt with the person of Jesus in his novel Midsummer Dance. The row over the novel finally ended up in court, which was not what

Simojoki had wanted. The young intelligentsia in Finland criticized heavily Simojoki's "outdated" view, and at the same time most conservative Christian groups saw his actions as rather too moderate.

From the early 1970s on Simojoki increasingly emphasized the churches' worldwide social responsibilities. He also became more ecumenically oriented, which he had not been as a young man. He played an important part in having the venue for the LWF's fifth assembly in 1970 moved from dictatorially ruled Brazil to France, showing even here his deep understanding of social ethical responsibility of the churches.

Simojoki was contemplative and fatherly, but also a skilled and diplomatic administrator. In addition, even as archbishop he retained his ability to take notice of individual people, regardless of their status, age, or sex. Even during his retirement Simojoki spoke in public at devotional events but kept his distance from the public discussion of church policy. He was thus wise enough to leave the leadership of the church to the younger generations.

AILA LAUHA

Urho Kekkonen: The Grand Man of Finland's Politics during the Cold War

Urho Kaleva Kekkonen, doctor of law and a member of the Center Party, was the most powerful post–World War II politician in Finland. His time as the president of the nation from 1956 to 1981 profoundly shaped Finland's political culture during the Cold War.

Kekkonen became politically active as a student of law at the University of Helsinki. He participated in student unions and politically affiliated sport associations, and he was one of the editors of *Ylioppilaslehti*, the student newspaper. Kekkonen was deeply influenced by Finnish nationalism, a popular movement among students during the 1920s and 1930s. After Finland gained its independence from Russia in 1917, the nationalists worked to build the young republic, secure the unity of its people after the civil war (1918), and replace Swedish, hitherto the official language of the country, with Finnish. Kekkonen joined in the last and successful efforts to establish Finnish as the language of teaching at the University of Helsinki, where courses had been traditionally offered in Swedish. As a member of the Academic Karelia Society, he took a hostile and suspicious stand toward the Soviet Union, but he stayed away from such radical right-wing movements as the Lapua Movement that stirred the country during the 1930s.

Kekkonen emerged in national politics during the 1930s when he was elected to parliament in 1936 and subsequently served as the Second Minister of Interior Affairs and as minister of justice. Nonetheless, Kekkonen gained prominence as the leading Finnish politician only after the Second World War; he served as prime minister between 1950 and 1956, and in 1956 he was dramatically elected president by only one vote.

President Kekkonen's stature as a leader of exceptional achievement was established during the perilous time between 1958 and 1961, when Cold War tensions seemed to imperil Finland's independence. Kekkonen, who engaged in active dialogue with the leaders of the Soviet Union, has been credited for securing Finland's neutrality. Many of his opponents saw him as a ruthless opportunist, but he was reelected in 1962 and 1968. In 1973 his term was prolonged with a mandate for four years, and in 1978, now seventy-eight years old, he was reelected once again through the regular election process. In 1981, however, his declining health forced him to resign in the middle of his term. He remained outside politics until his death in 1986.

Kekkonen was internationally known for his statesmanship, which secured Finland its independence without ignoring its geopolitical reality as a small country neighboring the powerful Soviet Union. Finland steadily developed as a Western democratic state both economically and culturally, and unlike many Eastern European countries, it was not occupied by Soviet forces or directly controlled by the Soviet Union. Nevertheless, in the Cold War era Finland was tied to its particular geopolitical circumstances, and international political crises between the East and the West created immediate insecurity and fear in Finns. It was particularly difficult to know whether the Soviet leaders would continue to trust Finland's neutrality and whether the Treaty of Friendship, Cooperation and Mutual Assistance, which the two countries signed in

1948, would stay in force. Since the collapse of the Soviet Union and the end of the Cold War, Kekkonen's politics of appeasement have been criticized both in Finland and abroad, but many Finns, especially the older generations who witnessed the Second World War and the perils of the Cold War, still regard them as prudent and realistic.

Kekkonen was a strong, charismatic personality who did not hesitate to exercise his power beyond traditional presidential parameters. He actively strove to influence not only parliamentary decision making but also regional politics, cultural life, and even the church.

Kekkonen observed particularly closely the events within the Evangelical Lutheran Church, to which an overwhelming majority of Finns belonged. The church had remained strongly patriotic and politically quite conservative since independence. Kekkonen saw the church's stance as reactionary and not appropriate for the political culture of the postwar period.

As president he had the power to confirm bishops after their election, but twice he ignored election results when he considered the winners too right-wing. He assigned the position to the person who was second in the elections. Such maneuvering angered many priests and bishops, many of whom had originally been against Kekkonen's presidency. In spite of this, later, especially since the early 1960s, Kekkonen succeeded in winning over the support of many leaders of the church. Bishops and priests grew particularly respectful of his foreign policy and came to see that he was the best choice for Finnish president in a world that faced the threat of nuclear war.

Kekkonen had warm personal relationships with a few bishops, but typically he kept a respectful distance from them in the 1950s and the 1960s. During the late 1960s and the 1970s he supported the young writers and artists who were shaped by the radical leftist ideals of the time and who parodied Christian morality and even religion. Kekkonen's interest in the affairs of the church declined notably at this time, but he always maintained polite relations with the Evangelical Lutheran Church that represented the majority of the Finns and thus had considerable, if indirect, political power. He never actively strove to weaken the position of the Lutheran church, knowing that such a move would anger many voters.

Privately Kekkonen seemed to have had a respectful attitude toward religion. His mother was a pious, practicing Christian. Kekkonen used some biblical citations in his political speeches, but for him they did not function as devotional statements but as catchy aphorisms.

Urho Kekkonen became a strong father figure to the Finns; his fierceness was softened by his good sense of humor and engaging personality. His long presidency is regarded positively by the leaders of today's church. The fact remains that Urho Kekkonen was influential in securing the independence of the Finnish nation and, with it, freedom of religion.

AILA LAUHA

Eivind Berggrav — Ecumenist and Church Leader

Eivind Berggrav is without doubt one of the most important church leaders in Norway in the twentieth century. As bishop of Oslo during World War II, he became the leader of the Norwegian *Kirchenkampf* against the Nazi government. After the war he was one of the leading ecumenists, influencing organizations like the WCC, the LWF, and the United Bible Societies.

Eivind Josef Jensen was born on October 25, 1884, in Stavanger, Norway, as son of Marena and Otto Jensen. In 1917 he changed his name to Eivind Berggrav, a family name from his grandmother. Otto was a pastor who later became bishop in the diocese of Hamar. As a theological student in Kristiania beginning in 1903, Eivind for a period had radical doubt about Christian faith, and the first years after his theological studies he did not want to practice as a pastor in the church. However, he became interested in the study of religious psychology, and after several visits to Germany (Marburg), Sweden (Lund), Denmark, and Great Britain (Cambridge), he finished a dissertation in 1924 (*Religionens terskel* [The threshold of religion]).

After ten years as a teacher and a journalist, he started as a parish pastor in 1919. Five years later he became a prison chaplain in Oslo, and then he was appointed bishop of the Hålogaland diocese in the north of

Norway. From 1929 on he and his wife Katherine (born Seip) lived in the city of Tromsø. In 1937 he became bishop of Oslo. Both his formal position as the country's leading bishop and his unique personal qualities brought him into the leadership in the church struggle against Nazism during World War II. In this struggle he succeeded in bringing together church leaders from different positions within Norwegian church life, cooperating with pietistic church leaders like Professor Ole Hallesby at Menighetsfakultetet (MF) and Ludvig Hope, the secretary-general of a radical low-church missionary organization.

As the central person behind the confession and declaration *Kirkens Grunn* (The foundation of the church) in April 1942, written as a defense of the church's refusal to cooperate with the Nazi government in Norway, Berggrav was arrested and held a prisoner in his own cabin outside of Oslo for three years. During these years he still was able to contact leaders within both the church and the resistance movement. He also wrote several books, among others a book on political ethics (*Staten og mennesket* 1945; English version, *Man and State,* 1951). In his struggle against Nazism and other totalitarian ideologies, Berggrav reinterpreted the Lutheran doctrine of the two kingdoms, stressing the duty to criticize and resist unjust authorities.

After the war he became more and more engaged in the ecumenical movement. In the late 1930s he had been a leader of the organization World Alliance for Promoting International Friendship through the Churches, and after the war he was actively involved in the planning process for the new WCC. He was one of the main speakers at the first General Assembly in 1948, talking about the witness of the churches in international affairs. He became a member of the central committee and the executive committee of the WCC, and from 1950 to 1954 was president of the organization. From 1947 on he also was the leader of the United Bible Societies.

In 1952 Berggrav gave a famous speech at the second General Assembly of the LWF in Hanover about state and church. After repeating his idea of the duty to resist unjust governments, he attacked the modern welfare states, claiming that they hid totalitarian tendencies. This accusation caused debate both in Germany and in Norway.

At the end of 1950 he resigned as bishop due to heart disease, but he was still active as an ecumenist and church leader both nationally and internationally until his death on January 14, 1959.

GUNNAR HEIENE

Gro Harlem Brundtland: "Norway's Radical Daughter"

During the last decades of the twentieth century, Gro Harlem Brundtland has been the most influential Norwegian leader both nationally and internationally. She was born on April 20, 1939, to a family deeply rooted in the Social Democratic movement. Her father was a medical doctor who specialized in rehabilitation medicine. For some years he worked in Egypt for the United Nations. Later he was appointed defense minister of the Norwegian cabinet, representing the Labour Party.

His daughter followed in her father's footsteps. In 1963 she became a medical doctor at the University of Oslo, and two years later she received a master of public health degree from Harvard University. For some years she worked for Oslo's Department of Social Services as the assistant medical director of the Oslo Board of Health, focusing on children's health issues.

In 1974 she became a member of the Labour government, serving as minister for environmental affairs until 1979. In 1981 she became Norway's first female prime minister, and appointed women to eight of the eighteen total positions in her cabinet. In September 1981 the Labour Party lost the election, and Brundtland became a leader of the opposition.

During these years she also broadened her international experience, as the leader of the World Commission on Environment and Development ("The Brundtland Commission"). The report called *Our Common Future* (1987) was internationally recognized as an important document, making the term "sustainable development" the focal point of discussions on environmental issues.

In April 1986 Brundtland returned to the prime ministership, serving until October 1989, and again from November 1990 until October 1996. In 1992 she resigned as leader of the Labour Party after the suicide of her son. As prime minister she initiated a modernizing process of the Norwegian welfare state. She proved to be a political leader with strong ambitions, inspired by her medical background. "There is a very close connection between being a doctor and a politician. The doctor tries to prevent illness, then tries to treat it if it comes. It's exactly the same as what you try to do as a politician, but with regard to society," she said according to a 1989 article in *Time* magazine on "Norway's radical daughter."

Brundtland has played an important role in the struggle for women's rights both nationally and internationally. She has underlined the need for empowering women through legislative changes, increased information, and redirection of resources. In the 1970s she lobbied for abortion rights in Norway, and as prime minister and leader of the Labour Party she gave priority to issues of gender equality, asserting that at least 40 percent of candidates on her party's ballot must be female.

In 1995 she spoke at the Fourth World Conference on Women in Beijing. Her international ambitions became more and more visible, and when she resigned as prime minister in 1996 there were rumors that she wanted to be UN secretary-general. This did not happen, but in 1998 she was elected the first female director general of the UN World Health Organization (WHO). As leader of the WHO in Geneva for five years, she had a unique opportunity to combine her medical and political experiences. She initiated a complete restructuring of the WHO and proved to be a strong and effective leader, focusing on issues like poverty and health care for women and children. She also started a campaign against the international tobacco industry, and in 2003 she coordinated a rapid worldwide response to the outbreaks of SARS. For this she was recognized by *Scientific American* as their Policy Leader of the Year.

GUNNAR HEIENE

Anders Nygren

Professor Anders Nygren was born in Gothenburg in western Sweden in 1890, where he grew up in a unique Christian atmosphere: one in which the church and its teachings on Martin Luther stood at the center of family life. Through all his years as a professor this emphasis never left him. Already at the age of twenty-one he had taken his theological exam at the University of Lund, and he later served as a minister in his home diocese.

He continued his studies even while serving as a minister. In 1921 he completed his doctoral dissertation, *Religious Apriori* (*Religiöst Apriori*, University of Lund, 1921). It deals with European philosophy, Kant, Schleiermacher, and academic theology. On religious experience he makes a distinction between reality and validity. In his greatest academic work, *Agape and Eros* (1930-36), he uses the method of motif research. Theology and particularly philosophy of religion should not be based on metaphysics, he asserts. The Christian understanding of love, described in the New Testament particularly by Saint Paul, was radically different from the Greek idealistic concept of love, eros, and also from that of the Jewish tradition in the Torah texts. *Agape and Eros* was a basic textbook for a generation of theologians in Sweden and Finland. It was translated into German, English, Spanish, and Chinese. It is probably the most widely circulated academic theological book of any Scandinavian in the twentieth century.

Through studies in Germany, Nygren got acquainted with many leading theologians. He married Irmgard Brandin, daughter of a Lutheran pastor in northern Germany. She was a theological partner to him as well, and helped with translation work. Nygren became well known in Germany, and was banned by the National Socialists in 1934. He received "Einreise- und Redeverbot," which meant that he could not travel or lecture.

Nygren was truly European in his outlook. At the end of the war he served in Norton Camp in Britain, giving theological lectures to prisoners of war. He also planned for the rebirth of the community of Lutherans. As a professor in Lund he was at the center of planning and implementing the general assembly at which the Lutheran World Federation (LWF) was founded in July 1947, and was chosen its first president. His keynote address finished with the words "Forward to Luther!" He also attended the assembly in Hanover in 1952. As president of LWF and as bishop of Lund from 1949 on, he visited churches in Tanganyika and South India.

Beginning in 1927, he was active in the Faith and Order meetings, at Lausanne, Edinburgh, and Oxford. He participated in the founding assembly of the World Council of Churches (WCC) in 1948 and the second one in Evanston in 1954. His main achievement in the ecumenical world might have occurred at the Faith and Order conference in Lund in 1952. With his academic and episcopal colleagues Yngve Brilioth and Gustaf Aulén, he led this conference. The report was entitled *Christ and the Church*. He perceived ecumenics as a deepening discovery of the gospel, not as a minimum leveler. Every church should look toward the center.

Academically, he was preoccupied with motif research on God's grace and love, and the theology of Luther. The history of the philosophy of religion was important to him. In an essay entitled "The Self-Evident in History" he discerned patterns of thinking and practice that were self-evident to the people of that time but were never documented and have lost their meaning to posterity.

At the height of Nygren's career in 1950, he and other theologians were strenuously attacked by proponents of logical positivism. Nygren was good in debate, but he was not attracted to slugging matches in defending his theological thoughts. He was accused of being unscientific. To secular, modern man, theology was not considered science and became marginalized.

In some ways the Lundensian theology of Nygren and Aulén was a counterweight to the dialectic theology of Karl Barth, which had great impact in Europe at the same time. In Sweden and Finland many clergy were taught the Lundensian theology and adopted it. In Lutheran seminaries in the United States and other parts of the world, Nygren was greatly appreciated. On October 20, 1978, Nygren died in the cathedral city of Lund, where he had spent most of his life as professor.

BJÖRN RYMAN

Olof Palme

Olof Palme (1927-86) was Swedish prime minister and chairperson of the Social Democratic Party from 1969 to his death; he was leader of the UN

Commission on Common Security, called the Palme Commission, and UN mediator on the Iran-Iraq war. He was murdered in Stockholm on February, 28, 1986.

Internationally, Palme is well known for his outspoken involvement on Third World issues, taking a stand for liberation and against oppression by the big powers. He was a leading critic of U.S. bombings against North Vietnam. This led to a cutoff of U.S.-Swedish diplomatic relations for four years.

Born into an upper-class family in Stockholm with German, Finnish, and Baltic roots, he attended private schools, which is rare in Sweden. He learned many languages and had a talent for delivering convincing speeches in them. As a student organizer, around 1950 he visited a student conference in Prague, which made him take an anticommunist stand. He did a year of college in the United States, which in one way impressed him but in another way made him conscious of the class and race struggle.

From student politics he was recruited to the office of Prime Minister Tage Erlander, who was the father figure of the long-reigning Social Democratic Party. He learned most of what he knew of the political trade during these years, which included a brief stint as minister for church affairs. The party promoted a "strong society" with a strong central power, which had the control of national economics as well as the means to develop the general welfare for all citizens. No private initiatives were allowed in the sectors of education, health, and care of the elderly.

Third World issues developed into a priority during Palme's days. Peace and justice issues on an international level were often high on the agenda. Willy Brandt and Bruno Kreisky were his European socialist counterparts. Both of them had been refugees in Sweden during the war. The Brandt commission on human development and the Palme commission on disarmament were twins of the same ideological school trying to create a new international economic order. In the beginning of the 1980s this might have worked as a political vision, but already when they were published they were politically dead. Swedish and Scandinavian development assistance reached 1 percent of GNP in these years. Palme — and Sweden — was particularly appreciated by the leaders of liberation movements in southern Africa and heads of state like Julius Nyerere of Tanzania. The small Central American countries also looked to Sweden during these years for support.

Palme gave the opening speech in April 1983 in Uppsala when, during an intense stage of the Cold War, Archbishop Olof Sundby invited 155 church leaders from all over the world to make a church contribution on the issue of disarmament. The theme was "Life and Peace," which is still the name of an ecumenical organization on conflict resolution based in Uppsala. Palme also spoke at WCC conferences.

As prime minister he made the political decision to postpone the church-state issue in 1972, when it approached decision stage in Parliament. This was a disappointment to the chairperson of this committee, Mrs. Alva Myrdal. It would take another twenty-five years until politicians and the public at large were ready for a consensus decision.

The murder of Palme by an unknown person on an open street in Stockholm while he walked with his wife without security guards shocked not only Sweden, but many in the world. Swedes lost their innocence after the murder. Most nations sent their foremost representatives to the funeral. He is buried in a churchyard in central Stockholm, close to the place of his death. The last rites at the funeral were performed by the bishop of Stockholm, Krister Stendahl, the well-known Harvard theologian.

Palme's wife, Lisbeth, a psychologist who specialized in children, continued to work on some of the issues close to her husband's heart. She did this as chairperson of UNICEF in Sweden, and has often spoken at church convocations on children's rights and justice issues.

The political agenda should be very different both domestically and internationally after Olof Palme. He was an agitator and leader for a new world order, but the world went in a different direction. A follower in his footsteps was Foreign Minister Anna Lindh (1957-2003). She was stabbed during a shopping walk in Stockholm and died on September 11, 2003. After two such open murders, Swedes ask themselves: When do we let our innocence go and wake up to the realities of the modern world?

BJÖRN RYMAN

Index of Persons

Index of Persons

FORSKNING FÖR KYRKAN
Church of Sweden ✠

1. Cecilia Wejryd, *Svenska kyrkans syföreningar 1844-2003*, 2005.
2. Björn Ryman, with Aila Lauha, Gunnar Heiene, and Peter Lodberg, *Nordic Folk Churches: A Contemporary Church History*. William B. Eerdmans Publishing Company, Grand Rapids, Michigan/Cambridge, U.K.